Stronger

The Daily Battle for Growth

Jai Haulk

Sermon to Book
www.sermontobook.com

Stronger / Jai Haulk
ISBN-13: 9780692728697
ISBN-10: 0692728694

To my wife, Angela, and to my kids Isaiah and Lucy. I want a stronger life so that I can be a more loving, encouraging, and servant-minded husband and father for you. And I want to do it to the best of my ability for as long as God will allow.

With thanks also to every family member, friend, and church that has pushed me to follow Jesus closer.

Acknowledgments

I want to extend special thanks and my deep appreciation to the following people for supporting my ministry in the publication of this book:

Josh and Anastasia Altar, Evan Anderson, Kyle Boots, Ed Brogden, Bruce and Susan Canal, Kristen and Phil Cubbage, Justen and Jessica Deck, Jason Elkins, Rick and Linda Elkins, Amy Ferguson, Brandon Grayson, Dustin Haulk, Martha Haulk, Raymond and Denise Haulk, Jena Jackson, David Keil, Jamie Keil, Daneisa Lain, Shaun McConnell, Jessica McLean, Kathleen Norton, Nancy Peters, Rich and Kim Phillips, Rick Shinkle, Neal Snapp, Bill and Michelle Thornburg, Lori Vaughan, and Julie Zaha.

CONTENTS

Note from the Author

Thank you for purchasing *Stronger: The Daily Battle for Growth.*

Accompanying each main chapter of the book is a set of reflective questions with a practical, application-oriented action step. These workbook sections are a tool to help you jumpstart your spiritual growth by further contemplating and applying the insights and lessons of each chapter.

I recommend you go through these workbook sections with a pen in order to write your thoughts and record notes in the areas provided. The questions are suitable for independent reflection, discussion with a friend, or review with a study group.

Regardless of what led you to this book or how you choose to approach it, I hope that the experience of reading and reflecting on it helps you understand more fully what it truly means to grow stronger in your walk with God.

INTRODUCTION

Strength Requires Change

I currently exercise at home, but before we had kids I used to exercise faithfully at a gym in town. After a while, I began to notice one guy specifically, and not in an awkward way.

Morning after morning I started watching him, because for being in the gym, he was doing something very strange. Maybe it was the fact that the man wasn't doing anything at all. While I was lifting, I would watch this guy check out the gym equipment. He looked at the leg extension machine to figure out how the pulley system worked on it. After somebody got done doing bench presses, this guy would walk over, check out how much each plate weighed, and count them up to see how much weight someone else was lifting. It became quite humorous.

This guy came in day after day; one day he read the newspaper, one day he talked to different people. He never lifted weights, never ran on the treadmill, and never rode an exercise bike. So I ask you, do you think he ever saw a physical change in his body? Of course not! He wasn't doing the exercise and the work that it takes to see any kind of physical progress.

So what happens when that starts to play out in our walk with Jesus? There's a difference between going to church and following Jesus. Going to church, you often get lots of information. There's a whole other step missing, though. Once we get the information, it's supposed to help change how we live outside of the church building. Information without application is useless. This is the way James, the brother of Jesus, phrased it:

> *But don't just listen to God's word. You must do what it says. Otherwise, you are only fooling yourselves. For if you listen to the word and don't obey, it is like glancing at your face in a mirror. You see yourself, walk away, and forget what you look like.* — ***James 1:22-24 (NLT)***

Who looks at a mirror in the morning to get ready for the day, then walks away and forgets what they look like? Nobody! That's absurd! The same goes for spiritual truth. It makes no sense to read the Bible or go to church and then walk away unchanged while not applying that truth to our day-to-day actions and words. I believe you can take one step even further. You can evaluate how effective a church service or Bible study was by the effect it had on your behavior and attitude that follows.

Did you ever think that we could go to church week after week and not see any change in our lives? I've seen it, and trust me: an immature fifty-year-old baby Christian isn't pretty. It's such a strange thing that someone can go to church for five, ten, twenty years and still not change.

And this book, *Stronger*, was written to make sure that doesn't happen to you. The central theme of this book is found in Acts:

> *The church...became stronger as the believers lived in the fear of the Lord.* — ***Acts 9:31 (NLT)***

Now I just want to clarify something from the beginning: The main theme of this book isn't saying that we can earn our salvation—because we can't. I don't care how hard you work, how many starving children you feed, how many Christmas gifts you get for the needy, or how strong you grow: You can't earn God's forgiveness or earn your way into heaven. This book is not about that at all. But salvation is freely given to anyone who calls on the name of Jesus, because what He did on the cross was enough to save you. Amen!

God's Plan for Your Life

A few months ago, I was in the middle of my exercise routine with a video. I had been working on the series *Les Mills Bodypump*, and one of the guys leading the exercise said something that made me literally stop in the middle of my workout. He said, "A stronger athlete is a better athlete." So simple, yet so true.

A stronger athlete is a better athlete, and a stronger Christian is a more effective Christian. Stronger Christians aren't just going to church—they're trying to let God's Word change their life. They're helping change the lives of other people around them. They're becoming more aware of what God is doing right in front of them every day. And they're jumping in to be his hands and feet.

We are going to look at several verses written by a guy named Paul, who at one point was killing Christians for their faith. Now he was sitting in prison for his faith in Jesus and writing these words:

> *I want to know Christ and experience the mighty power that raised him from the dead. I want to suffer with him, sharing in his death, so that one way or another I will experience the resurrection from the dead!* — ***Philippians 3:10-11 (NLT)***

Now go back and reread those verses with some serious passion! Paul saw these things that he needed to experience in his life as a necessity. He had to experience God's power. He had to go through suffering and understand the death of Jesus. He saw these changes in his life as necessary because he knew that God's plan for our lives is to grow us to be stronger.

The Necessity of Change

So let's just pretend for a minute that you are a mechanic (for some of you I know that's a stretch). And let's say I brought this motorcycle into your shop. And I say, "Um, it's running rough. It's got a pretty bad vibration while I'm going down the road. And every time I get above one hundred, things just start flying and I'm just not sure what's wrong it."

And you, as the professional mechanic, would say to me: "You have a flat tire. And if you fix the flat tire, then I think you'll have fixed the problem."

What if I said back, "Nah, I think what it needs is a new paint job. It's because it's blue. What if we painted it the color orange? Then I'd just feel better about it." You'd reply, "You can paint your motorcycle hot pink for all I care. It doesn't matter what color you paint it; the bike isn't going to run effectively until you fix the tire."

Then I would say: "No, I don't think the tire's the problem. I think if we installed a sweet new stereo system it would be so much better." You'd tell me: "Hey man! You can install an eight-track player in it for all I care, but until you change that flat tire, it's never going to run to its potential."

We have to see change as necessary. And to grow, we must change our flat tires. Moses saw change as necessary and led God's people out of Egypt. Joshua saw change as necessary and led God's people into the Promised Land. Nehemiah saw change as necessary and helped Jerusalem rebuild its walls. Paul, after meeting

Jesus, saw change as necessary. He was a religious leader going around killing Christians, but changed into the guy who wrote the majority of the New Testament. Jesus obviously saw change as necessary, being willing to die to save all mankind from staying forever separated from God.

> *I don't mean to say that I have already achieved these things or that I have already reached perfection. But I press on to possess that perfection for which Christ Jesus first possessed me. No, dear brothers and sisters, I have not achieved it. —* ***Philippians 3:12-13 (NLT)***

Paul had the whole Old Testament memorized, and He followed the Jewish law almost to perfection. And what did Paul say about himself? "I've not achieved it yet."

If Paul wasn't there yet and still wanted more, and still saw the need for change in his life, then how much more do we need it? And this doesn't really mean that he will ever achieve perfection: It means that he's constantly pursuing this idea of continually perfecting himself to look more like Jesus.

Lasting Change—Not a One-Time Project

Imagine you want to start a new hobby or pick up a new sport. So you go out and pick up what you need in expectation of being really good at it within a few hours—even though it has taken other people a long process of daily practice to get there.

This concept can be applied to losing weight. We want to lose weight, so we go on a diet. But what we need is to be eating the right food and to be involved in some type of physical activity every day. It's a daily process, not a one-time project. We need to get used to the fact that one-time quick fixes will never last.

The challenge for many of us who have already been Christian for a while now is that we sometimes feel like we've arrived. We've got some Bible verses memorized. We went on a mission trip to a third-world country, or we helped with some service projects. We've got this whole Jesus thing down pat. Again, this goes back to seeing faith like a project. Just checking items off the list as you get them done. But it's so much more than that. It's a daily, moment-by-moment pursuit. It's inviting God into your everyday moments of success and failure.

> *...but I focus on this one thing: Forgetting the past and looking forward to what lies ahead.* — **Philippians 3:13 (NLT)**

Forget the Past, Look to the Future

I'm not talking about not learning from past mistakes. That still needs to happen. Rather, I'm talking about the things of our past that are always looking to haunt us.

For me, I want to be a stronger, better dad. But Satan continues to remind me of this one moment where my parenting skills were definitely lacking. It's been about a year ago now, but one day, my then three-year-old son Isaiah had thrown so many fits and tantrums that it had worn me down. I can't even remember what finally pushed my last button. But by the end of the meltdown, I'm ashamed to say I had taken his three-foot-tall plastic Batman toy and smashed it over his clothing dresser. Both his new action figure and the new giraffe head knobs on the dresser remind me of this moment of failure.

What's in your past that you can't seem to let go of? Label it. Then repeat this phase over and over to yourself until it sinks in: The pain of my past doesn't determine my future!

Martin Luther King, Jr. said, "If you can't fly then run, if you can't run then walk, if you can't walk then crawl, but whatever you do you have to keep moving forward."[1]

If I could sit down and have coffee with each one of you—first off I might end up in a sugar coma because I drink those fancy coffees, lattes with whipped cream and caramel drizzles. Second, I'd tell each one of you the same thing Dr. King said: Don't give up. Don't give up! I know there are days, months, or even years where things look bleak, and you're questioning where God is and what he's doing in your life that involves these circumstances. But no matter how bad our circumstances get, it doesn't change God's goodness. God is good. Don't give up on the God who hasn't given up on you! Paul wrote:

> *...I press on to reach the end of the race and receive the heavenly prize for which God, through Christ Jesus, is calling us.* — ***Philippians 3:14 (NLT)***

Paul used a unique phrase here: He said that he "presses on"; that is, he kept moving forward with life in a gritty kind of way, which is the entire focus of the next chapter. But he went on to say:

> *Let all who are spiritually mature agree on these things. If you disagree on some point, I believe God will make it plain to you. But we must hold on to the progress we have already made.* — ***Philippians 3:15-16 (NLT)***

There are loads of spiritual truths in these verses, but one is especially crucial: the idea of spiritual maturity, which first implies that there are those who are spiritually immature, and second, that there's progress to be made. Living stronger requires change. We must develop strength in areas of life where we are weak.

So what does that look like for you? As we move forward, this book will focus on the areas of grit, Bible study, emotions, relationships, mental health, finances, physical health, and living out our priorities. Before continuing, take an educated guess about yourself: In which area(s) does something need to change in order for you to live stronger in the fear of the Lord?

WORKBOOK

Introduction Questions

Question: In what ways have you seen your behaviors and attitudes change since becoming a Christian? In what ways do you want to become a more effective Christian?

____

____

____

____

____

____

____

____

____

____

____

____

Question: How are you allowing the Word to change you? How are you responding to the messages you hear at church?

Question: What changes are necessary in your everyday life in order for God to do great things through you as He did with Moses, Joshua, Nehemiah, and Paul? How can you grow stronger?

____

____

Action: God needs to be involved in your everyday moments of success and failure. Invite Him into your day and your life so He can show you the changes you need to make in order to live stronger. I challenge you to pray this prayer:

"God, where do You want to use me today? Who needs something from me? Amen."

Then be looking for His answer.

Introduction Notes

CHAPTER ONE

Growing Grit

Recently, the ministry staff I serve with went to a leadership conference called the Global Leadership Summit put on by Willow Creek Community Church. Pastor Bill Hybels opened up the first session by talking about the leadership qualities it would take to move businesses or ministries from where they are now to where they need to be. One of the top five leadership qualities he listed was the idea of grit. Then, at the end of the message, he told us about the grit test on Willow Creek's website. My lead pastor leaned over to me and said, "I bet you would score high on that test." I remember taking that as a compliment—I don't remember scoring high on too many tests in my life. But he ended up being right.

The continued focus of this book is to ensure we understand God's plan for us to grow stronger once we have become a follower of Jesus. We find that in several areas of Scripture, but Luke stated it well in the book of Acts:

> *The church...became stronger as the believers lived in the fear of the Lord. —* ***Acts 9:31 (NLT)***

If we aren't growing in the different areas of our life—relationships, emotions, thought life, finances, or even our physical health—we are doing something wrong. Growing isn't going to be easy. But this is where grit comes in.

What Is Grit?

Psychologist Angela Lee Duckworth has put a great deal of study into this idea of grit. She states that grit is "the ability to persevere in pursuing a future goal over a long period of time and not giving up...It is having stamina. It's sticking with your future, day-in, day-out, not just for the week, not just for the month, but for years, and working really hard to make that future a reality. Grit is living life like it's a marathon, not a sprint."[2] Or in terms of this book, to have grit means to grow stronger. Grit is a kind of toughness—not in a prideful or egotistical way, but in endurance and zeal.

> *I press on to reach the end of the race and receive the heavenly prize for which God, through Christ Jesus, is calling us. —* ***Philippians 3:14 (NLT)***

The original Greek word Paul used in the phrase "I press on" brings with it a similar idea of pursuing the end of the race aggressively, and to pursue it through any persecution that comes. It's a form of toughness—an exceptional willingness to get back up and finish after being knocked down again and again.

Grit is not being content merely to exist with the status quo. Now, don't get me wrong: There are times and ways in which we ought to be content with our life. I'm not promoting buying the sixty-two-inch TV because the fifty-five-inch just wasn't good enough. I'm talking about the desire to push yourself and challenge your peers.

In our staff calendar meeting last year, my lead pastor revealed our new church theme for 2016. It was a focus on the Holy Spirit. He talked us through the plans for the year, which sounded great and exciting. Then he proceeded to show us the artwork that would hang on the foyer wall for the year. Now I can't speak for everyone in the room, but at that point I lost all enthusiasm. It simply didn't inspire me, and the church is in the inspiration business.

He asked for our opinions. A few said it was okay and they liked it. Then, for better or worse, I stated that I hated it and laid out my reasoning. My desire wasn't to be disrespectful. If I can't be honest with the church staff I'm working with, then with whom can I be honest? Plus, people who know me find out that honesty is a core value of my life. Yes, it gets me in trouble from time to time, but there's something inside of me that says anything less than our best just doesn't cut it.

Where Do We See Grit in Scripture?

As I read through Scripture, the word "grit" never shows up. Yet you see it in the lives of people throughout the Bible whom God has used to grow His kingdom. At first glance, you'll notice that each of these people were broken, flawed, and jacked-up human beings—just like myself. But they showed grit in how they lived out their life.

Take Noah, for example, in Genesis chapters 6 and 7. Noah endured years of building a boat in the middle of nowhere, in an area that didn't flood, waiting for this promise of God. Meanwhile, other people likely made fun of him and his family. Then—even scarier—he was stuck on a boat for over twelve months with only his family and the animals. That, my friends, is a recipe for chaos. Some of us can barely pull off the holidays without wanting to strangle a family member!

And what about Joseph, the father of Jesus? Talk about grit. This guy planned a typical engagement and marriage with his fiancée Mary, only to find out she was pregnant. And not only was she not pregnant by him, she was pregnant by God. Angels talked to him. Kings tried killing his family because the newborn baby was rumored to be a future king. He endured with patience and wisdom through it all. Of course, being a young father myself, I have discipline issues with my kids. How difficult must it have been to discipline the Son of God?

Then you have Abraham, who rescued his nephew Lot from some rather nasty situations. Moses and Joshua had to lead a relocation project of about one million people to the Promised Land. Jacob's son Joseph went from being his father's favorite, to being thrown in a pit by his own brothers, being sold into slavery, living in prison—staying faithful until his moment came—and then being asked to save his family, who had betrayed him. Rahab hid the spies against her governing authorities. Esther stood up for her people, knowing she risked death by going before the king. Nehemiah had the passion and discipline to lead the people to rebuild the city walls amidst critics and bandits. The list of gritty men and women from Scripture goes on and on.

Why Do We Need Grit?

We need grit because God created you on purpose, for a purpose, to live a life honoring Him and making disciples. But doing this in a world that hates you and doesn't understand your purpose isn't going to be easy.

> *But to you who are willing to listen, I say, love your enemies! Do good to those who hate you.* — ***Luke 6:27 (NLT)***

If you've ever been told that Christianity is about your happiness, or just a way to get into heaven, you've been sold a load of garbage. God is not against your happiness. And yes, Jesus is the way to heaven. But when you read the words of Jesus, you can see that those two things aren't the bottom line. I don't know about your bucket list, but loving my enemies and doing good to those who hate me aren't on mine for the sake of my happiness. They're on it because Jesus said so, and I'm going to need grit to accomplish them.

An example of this was demonstrated by Martin Luther King, Jr. in the middle of one of his peace rallies: A KKK member rushed the stage and began to just pummel King. Rally supporters then began to jump this guy, and things quickly became ugly. King ended up getting between his attacker and his own people to protect the guy who had just assaulted him. As things calmed down, King began singing worship songs and introduced the guy to his followers as if the man were his guest. That's just not normal. That kind of response in a heated situation takes a unique kind of toughness.

If Jesus's command in Luke 6:27 wasn't enough to convince you, then read on—He was notorious for making tough, challenging statements, as in Luke 14:26:

> *If you want to be my disciple, you must hate everyone else by comparison—your father and mother, wife and children, brothers and sisters—yes, even your own life. Otherwise, you cannot be my disciple.* ***(NLT)***

Now does Jesus really desire that you hate your mother and father? Of course not. Why would God set up the entire family faith system in the first five books of the Bible only to tear it apart later? That makes no sense. Rather, Jesus was trying to make the point that it's going to be extremely difficult to be His disciple. He hints at the idea that grit is going to be required if you are going to grow and be an effective disciple.

One of the reasons why we should develop grit is that grit has proven to be more effective than either IQ or talent. Our culture puts a high priority on natural talent and on being smart. But those things have proven to fail or have been wasted when someone doesn't have the gritty endurance to push through when things get tough.

If you answer yes to any of these questions, you're going to need to develop grit in your life.

- Do you have a lifestyle habit that needs to change for your future physical health?
- Have you finally made up your mind to rid yourself of that addiction?
- Are you a parent?
- Do you desire for your business or ministry to go to the next level?
- Are you in any position of life where you are leading other people?

How to Grow Grit—for Ourselves and Our Kids

Share gritty stories. One way we learn is by hearing past examples of people's perseverance. Obviously, there are lots of biblical examples and people from history. Keep in mind there are also examples not only from America's history—such as Abraham Lincoln—but also from stories within your own family.

Do something that is physically tough for you. Physically experiencing something helps to develop a memory of something gritty to recall for years to come.

When we can remember doing something tough in our past, it encourages future gritty activity.

Allow kids to be a part of a problem-solving process in your life. Too often we find the need to protect our kids from adult issues. Obviously, this comes with using your discretion about what you think your child can handle, depending on their age and maturity. If you start having a struggle at work, talk about it at home and let your kids offer suggestions. Or maybe something is needed for a family member or friend and the finances just aren't there. In this case, let kids be a part of the solution by working out a fundraising idea or getting a part-time job, which teaches them to endure by problem-solving.

Talk about and work through your fears. Eleanor Roosevelt said, "Do one thing every day that scares you."[3] Fear keeps us in our comfort zone, and it holds us back from chasing our dreams. Overcoming our fears, however, develops courage.

Teach self-control. Self-control develops grit because it's a discipline learned over time. This means not blurting out a negative comment even when you want to. Self-control is saving money and not impulse-buying.

Set up tough life experiences. As Bill Hybels stated at the Global Leadership Summit, "Grit development demands difficulty."

For instance, growing up, my brother and I would gather a few other guys to get together and play different sports depending on the season. It was more like we gathered the other four guys who lived in the village of

Browns Valley, Indiana. We'd team up and play flag football, which typically turned to tackle after about five minutes. This was fun when it was nice and warm out, but deep down I think every one of us would have told you we preferred it to be either raining or snowing. There was something exhilarating about being annihilated only to stand back up covered in mud, or about trying to catch a football while your hands were frozen solid. It was fun, yet messy and painful.

Angela Duckworth's family has put in place something called the *Hard Thing Rule*. This helps their young daughters to experience grit. The Hard Thing Rule is that everyone in the family must be doing something that is difficult. Of course they want it be something they have an interest in—ballet, a musical instrument, archery—but the key requirements are that it must require almost daily practice, and that they can't quit. It doesn't matter if they're bored or don't feel they're good at it. They can revisit their choice if they want to change their hard thing at the end of the semester or school year, but not before.

Angela says, "I believe kids should choose what they want to do, because it's their life, but they have to choose something," she says. "And they can't quit in the middle unless there's a really good reason. There are going to be peaks and valleys. You don't want to let kids quit during a valley."

As parents or grandparents, we need to be more aware of how we are guiding or disciplining the next generation. Gone are the days of "Do as I say, not as I do." Thankfully, young people are wise enough not to buy into that lie. No matter what you want to invest in them, you are actually investing who you are at the core into them. You're investing in them through the behaviors and life attributes you live out every day in front of them. Your kids are watching you as you handle your relationships, finances, behavior, and goals. As you guide and discipline your kids, do you invoke God and the church to grind them down, or do you lead them to Him?

Thinking Big—Thinking Mud Puddles

One last area in which you need to develop grit is in challenging small-minded thinking. If the complaint "we've never done it that way before" is a common utterance for you, then it's time for something new. In the book of Isaiah, chapter 43, God reminded His people of the good things He had done for them in their past. Then he stopped and did this U-turn:

> *But forget all that—it is nothing compared to what I am going to do. For I am about to do something new. See, I have already begun!* — ***Isaiah 43:18-19 (NLT)***

I love the way God spoke through Isaiah here. In effect, he said, "the past was great, but forget all that because what I'm going to do is new and will blow you away!" The past is nothing compared to what God still wants to do with you. Your age or life demographic doesn't matter. God has already started something new inside of you, and it's going to take grit to bring it to fruition.

My challenge to you is, the next time you think or say the words, "I can't do that," stop right there and resolve to do exactly what you thought you couldn't. I don't care what it is—do it.

Living out this challenge will be different for every single person who chooses to grow grit. Maybe your friend invites you to run a mini-marathon together. Instead of coming up with excuses for why you can't do it, start the process of training so you can run or even walk it. When a need for a new ministry comes up, instead of focusing on the struggles necessary to make it happen, envision the rewards of what could be. Don't over-complicate things. Just do the next thing needed to make it happen.

Before I learned about grit, I used to hate the idea of walking outside in the rain or getting my hands dirty. It seriously bugged me. If my kids were walking toward a puddle, I made them avoid it by grabbing their arms and jumping them over it. Now we find puddles to splash in! Now I encourage it.

What puddle do you need to step in? Or better yet, what puddle do you need to jump into so it splashes all over your kids or grandkids. It's time to develop grit in your life. Without grit, we lose heart. Without grit, we walk away from the challenges God puts in front of us. Without grit, we settle for less than God's best.

WORKBOOK

Chapter One Questions

Question: In your relationships, do you walk away when things get messy? During the hard times of life, are you always the victim? Do you easily give into cravings or addictions? In what areas of life do you need to develop grit?

Question: What goals, ideas, and attitudes have your kids or grandkids seen you follow through on and complete? How can you model grit for them?

Question: What hard thing that scares you but honors God are going to begin doing daily? How? What small steps will you take each day?

____

____

____

Action: Grow in practicing your faith by learning to demonstrate grit in your daily life. Take the words of Jesus and the examples in Scripture seriously, and do difficult things, fearing only God. Challenge small-minded thinking as you live out God's purposes for you, and train your children to face life with the same grit you do. Take the grit test and see just how gritty you are (http://angeladuckworth.com/grit-scale/)!

Chapter One Notes

CHAPTER TWO

Stronger Spiritually

Feeling the call of God in my life, I started Bible college at Lincoln Christian University in 2001. But I'll admit that an event that took place a couple of days after the freshmen moved onto campus caught me off guard. They sat all of the incoming freshman in the biggest room they could find and said, "We are going to take an 'introduction to the Bible' exam."

At first I thought, "Okay, this can't be too bad. I mean, I helped lead some Bible studies while in high school, right?" I leaned over in my seat to get the attention of one of the professors and asked, "Hey, um, by chance do you know which part of the Bible we're being tested on?" Her answer raised my anxiety level a few notches: "Oh, you're going to cover the whole thing."

"You've got to be kidding me!" I groaned inwardly. It was definitely one of those moments when God was laughing at me. "Yeah," I thought, "I guess I should've read Your Bible more, huh?"

I don't remember the exact number, but my percentage on the test was somewhere in the range of twenty to thirty percent. It was not one of the moments that made my momma's highlight reel.

The good news is that they gave us a chance to redeem ourselves in our senior year, when we took the same test again. My second attempt was rather better, with a score between eighty and ninety percent—which still wasn't where I wanted to be, but I'll take that kind of score over flunking any day.

But what happens when someone has been a Jesus follower for years, yet would flunk an intro to the Bible exam? I love how one my Bible professors, J. K. Jones, would have answered: "A dusty Bible leads to a dirty life." He taught me to crave God's Word.

So far we've been talking about the idea of growing stronger—about how (after we become a believer) we have to work through the process to become a stronger and more effective Christian. Our main verse in this regard is from Acts chapter 9.

> *The church...became stronger as the believers lived in the fear of the Lord. —* ***Acts 9:31 (NLT)***

You may be playing devil's advocate with me right now and thinking, "Do I really need to know the Bible? Can't I just live the greatest commandments like Jesus stated? You know, 'Love God and love others?' That's enough to get into heaven, so why worry about the rest?" The thing is, though, if you truly love someone, you want to know what they have to say. And God spoke volumes to humanity through Scripture.

God showed one of His prophets, Ezekiel, some lessons about this, according to Ezekiel chapter 37. However, God chose to do this in rare fashion and with some special effects that would bring amazement even to today's filmmakers:

> *The LORD took hold of me, and I was carried away by the Spirit of the LORD to a valley filled with bones. He led me all around among the bones that covered the valley floor. They were scattered everywhere across the ground and were completely dried out.* — **Ezekiel 37:1-2 (NLT)**

We all experience spiritually dry places. God led Ezekiel into the desert. Where's your dry place?

Maybe it's a family gathering where the conversation is anything but godly. Or a company softball team that likes to drink a little too much. Not to mention the friend who believes that politics will save the world.

But just as God led Ezekiel by the hand to that dry place for a reason, He has done the same for you. You're with your family, at your job location, or interacting with those friends for a reason. For what reason did God lead Ezekiel out to the desert?

> *Then he asked me, "Son of man, can these bones become living people again?" "O Sovereign LORD," I replied, "you alone know the answer to that."* — **Ezekiel 37:3 (NLT)**

Ezekiel might have wondered: "Is that a trick question, God?" But Ezekiel knew that you don't tell the God of the universe "no," so he gave the wise answer, "I don't know, God. But I'm sure you do."

> *Then he said to me, "Speak a prophetic message to these bones..."* — ***Ezekiel 37:4 (NLT)***

If I were Ezekiel right then, I would've been praying that nobody passed by on their camel or they'd be taking me to the nuthouse for sure! Talking to bones? Yet who would be bringing the bones back to life: Ezekiel, the dry bones themselves, or God?

> *Then he said to me, "Speak a prophetic message to these bones and say, 'Dry bones, listen to the word of the LORD! This is what the Sovereign LORD says: Look! I am going to put breath into you and make you live again! I will put flesh and muscles on you and cover you with skin. I will put breath into you, and you will come to life. Then you will know that I am the LORD.'"* — ***Ezekiel 37:4-6 (NLT)***

That's right: God.

> *So I spoke this message, just as he told me. Suddenly as I spoke, there was a rattling noise all across the valley. The bones of each body came together and attached themselves as complete skeletons. Then as I watched, muscles and flesh formed over the*

> *bones. Then skin formed to cover their bodies, but they still had no breath in them.* — **Ezekiel 37:7-8 (NLT)**

Hold up. Somebody call the SyFy channel! And here I thought snakes were the only thing that could make me run screaming like a little schoolgirl.

> *Then he said to me, "Prophesy to the breath; prophesy, son of man, and say to it, 'This is what the Sovereign LORD says: Come, breath, from the four winds and breathe into these slain, that they may live.'" So I prophesied as he commanded me, and breath entered them; they came to life and stood up on their feet—a vast army.* — **Ezekiel 37:9-10 (NIV)**

The only thing that can bring someone from spiritual death to life is God's Word. Scripture is what will make us stand up strong. Ezekiel preached God's Word over the dry bones, and they came to life. I can't emphasize enough the importance of the Bible for each person's spiritual growth.

We must learn to feed ourselves from God's Word.

Spiritual Adults or Spiritual Babies?

In the student ministry I lead, I could easily just read through some scriptures, straight up hand the students the spiritual answers they need, and tell them how to apply those truths to their lives. That's what ministries have done for students and adults alike for years. But I believe such an approach hinders their spiritual growth.

The problem then becomes that they can't read, question, and apply the Scriptures for themselves. They'll live their entire life looking to a pastor or other church leader to grow them spiritually when they should be doing much of it on their own at home. I vow not to let that happen. I don't want to be known for raising spiritual babies, as Paul mentions in 1 Corinthians:

> *Dear brothers and sisters, when I was with you I couldn't talk to you as I would to spiritual people. I had to talk as though you belonged to this world or as though you were infants in the Christ. I had to feed you with milk, not with solid food, because you weren't ready for anything stronger.* — **1 Corinthians 3:1-2 (NLT)**

Apparently, Paul picked up on what we can still see in the church today. There are spiritual babies who believe in Jesus but who aren't growing stronger to maturity because they live by their own worldly desires. So at some point, each of us must ask ourselves how much influence our worldly desires have on us. Our goal should be that God's desires would become our desires, and the only way for that to happen is to read the Scriptures and find the heartbeat of God.

How to Study God's Word

If there's a right way to do something, then there's also a way not to do it. Yes, there's a wrong way to read Scripture. And not only is there a wrong way to read it, but doing so can also be extremely dangerous. Paul says this to the church of Ephesus regarding the proper understanding of Scripture:

> *Then we will no longer be immature like children. We won't be tossed and blown about by every wind of new teaching. We will not be influenced when people try to trick us with lies so clever they sound like the truth. Instead, we will speak the truth in love, growing in every way more and more like Christ, who is the head of his body, the church.* — ***Ephesians 4:14-15 (NLT)***

The million-dollar Bible college word that is used to make sure we are not being tricked by what sounds like truth is "hermeneutics." By definition, hermeneutics refers to our method of studying the Scriptures for application to our lives today. Why does this matter? As I mentioned earlier, not sticking to a specific method of studying Scripture is very dangerous. For centuries, people have twisted scriptures to further agendas that couldn't be any further from God. Too often, we are tempted to let our emotions or life experiences affect the truth that we read on a given day.

Which Bible?

Reading Scripture is ultimately about asking the right questions, and one of the most common questions I get as a pastor is "What version should I be reading?"

I remember one Sunday morning when a student in my ministry blurted out, "I've tried reading the Bible, but I just can't understand it." I asked what version he was reading, and it was the New King James version. I went to the closet in the youth room and grabbed him an NLT (New Living Translation) version out of the stash that I always keep on hand for students. "This should help," I let him know.

Personally, I also recommend getting a study Bible—NLT, NIV (New International Version), or ESV (English Standard Version). If you're not using a devotional or other resources, a good study Bible is extremely helpful. Go to your local Christian bookstore and spend some time looking through different options to see what kind of notes you like. Some versions mention more information about the cultural background of what is happening in the passage you're reading. Others focus more on application. Currently, I'm loving the Bible Study App by Olive Tree—I have multiple versions of the Bible, and if I highlight a passage or copy down notes, they appear no matter which version I'm using. I also purchase other Christian books that stay within the same app. So while I'm reading Andy Stanley's book *The Grace of God*, I can also see the scriptures about grace at the same time.

What's the Whole Story?

In Stephen Covey's book *The 7 Habits of Highly Effective People*, he shared a story of a train ride he had experienced.[4] On the train was a father of three kids. They were literally bouncing off the seats—and off of a few passengers as well. I'm not exactly the confrontational type, but Covey got to the point where he had to do something. He told the father, "Sir, your children are really disturbing a lot of people. I wonder if you couldn't control them a little more?" The dad glanced at him and replied, "Oh, you're right. I guess I should do something about it. We just came from the hospital where their mother died about an hour ago. I don't know what to think, and I guess they don't know how to handle it, either." Covey, along with others I'm sure, made assumptions without understanding the background to what was going on.

Our temptation is to read a passage and jump straight to how it applies today. But first we have to understand what was taking place culturally when it was first written. We do this because the writing was first intended for that time and place. When Paul talks about not eating sacrificial meat, we need to know the cultural background to understand the point he's trying to make to them. Only then can we understand what that means to us.

What Sticks Out?

What's jumping out at you from Scripture? Is there anything strange—like Jesus cursing a fig tree? Are there any repeated words or themes? Are two things being compared, such as darkness and light? These are the things to which you should pay special attention. It's no different than observing what the person next to you is eating for lunch. It's being aware of what's going on in the text. If questions come up, write them down.

How Do We Use This?

From the observations you've made, you'll be able to pull out God's truths for you to live by. Have a journal handy and write them down. Then get even more specific on how you're planning to apply them to your daily life: "Pray for my enemies"—that's a good start. Now list them by name and pray for one each day over the next week.

Studying the Bible is just like anything else in life: you're going to have to do your part and work at it if you want to grow.

> *So get rid of all evil behavior. Be done with all deceit, hypocrisy, jealousy, and all unkind speech. Like newborn babies, you must crave pure spiritual milk so that you will grow into a full experience of salvation. Cry out for this nourishment...* — ***1 Peter 2:1-2 (NLT)***

If you don't crave God's Word in the way that this scripture describes, then beg Him to renew your passion. Grow stronger through study! Asking the right questions is a good place to start.

WORKBOOK

Chapter Two Questions

Question: When have you let your emotions or experiences affect your interpretation of Scripture? How did God eventually correct your understanding of the Scripture in question?

Question: How often do you study Scripture? What is your level of desire to read Scripture daily? How, specifically, can you grow stronger in this regard?

Question: What is your specific plan for studying the Scriptures to spiritually grow stronger?

Action: God's Word gives life. Don't underestimate the importance of reading Scripture daily. Remember also that there are right ways and wrong ways to read Scripture. Resist the urge to apply a scripture immediately to your life or to base your interpretation on your own emotions and current life experiences. Take the time instead to pick a study Bible in a translation you understand and to access information about the historical context of the scriptures you read. Study God's Word daily and you will grow stronger from the spiritual nourishment that the Scriptures provide!

Chapter Two Notes

CHAPTER THREE

Stronger Emotionally

Our church has an Amazon Prime account, and over the last few years we have seemed to be a new hub for Amazon packages. One morning as I cracked open my office door, I saw an Amazon box sitting on my desk. I love it when this happens. I mean, who doesn't love getting packages? Sometimes I even forget what I ordered, between ministry products for the youth group and personal stuff for home. It's hard to keep track. It's almost like a mini-Christmas—and I love Christmas! On this particular day, I opened the box and found a Bible inside. It was like finding life in a box!

Then I started thinking more about the *Inside Out* movie from Pixar that I had watched with my kids. As much as they liked it, it really wasn't meant for four- and five-year-olds. It's a film that follows one little girl's life as interpreted by her different personified emotions. In the control room of the brain, where the emotions hang out, is an area where the memories are stored.

I started to think how cool it would be if Amazon collected your emotions and memories all day long; then, upon your arrival home from work, a box from Amazon would be waiting there for you. Each day you could open up your box, and inside would be your day—all of the moments you had experienced and the emotions attached to them. This would be life-changing. And yes, I'll expect a cut if anyone sells this idea to Amazon.

True to the movie, emotions are a major way in which we analyze life as it comes at us. The lights go out, or we hear the word "bomb," and fear sets in. We experience the death of a loved one and our heart breaks with sadness. Our dog eats its own vomit and disgust rises up. In such ways, our emotions are how we experience life—but what happens when they seem to take over our life?

Emotions were created to be godly; sin has made them selfish. We can look at every emotion we have and see a part of God's character, but then we can see how sin twists it into something worldly and selfish—used for our own desires.

We get angry because something we feel entitled to is taken away from us. But God gets angry about people being taken advantage of.

Fear in the world comes from gunshots, or because we feel a lack of security in our lives from a dramatic event. But fear was created so we would respect God's authority.

We get disgusted and judge someone who offends us, but God gets disgusted when our faith and the way we live our lives don't match up.

Relationship over Rules

Next, we are going to glance into the life of a guy for whom God had great plans, but whose emotions took over his life. His name was Samson. You find a lot of his life story in the book of Judges in the Bible. Most likely, you know some of the more notorious things about him.

First, the dude was strong. Like, Dwayne "The Rock" Johnson strong. You don't mess with this guy; or if you do, you'd better pray you can run faster than him—that kind of strong.

Second, maybe you've heard the story of Samson and Delilah. The source of Samson's strength was partially due to his hair, but he was only blessed with that because his family had made very specific promises. They were called Nazarite vows, including these three parts found in the book of Numbers chapter 6.

1. No drinking wine or any drink from the vine
2. No cutting their hair
3. No touching anything dead

Some of us look at that and think: "What's with all of the rules? I have enough restrictions in life, but these people wanted more? Why would anybody do this?" Where you see rules, however, they saw a better life—a unique life of blessing from God.

Maybe you're someone who thinks that God just wants to restrict you—that He just wants to suck the fun out of it all—and for this reason you haven't given your life over to Jesus and been baptized. If you're simply not sold on the idea of giving your whole life plans over to the God of the universe yet, forget the rules. Just forget them. Because as you forget about the rules, you begin to read the Bible with a different mindset. And as you do that, you'll begin to see that God cares more about your heart and more about a relationship with you than he does about the rules.

Unfortunately, there some Christians who struggle to let go of the rules. Sadly, they become legalistic, thinking they can somehow earn more of God's love and acceptance when He already freely gives it.

With this in mind, let's return to Samson's story. Samson dedicated his life to God. He had made promises and vows that were designed to keep his life on track, but watch what his emotions did to him:

> *One day when Samson was in Timnah, one of the Philistine women caught his eye. When he returned home, he told his father and mother, "A young Philistine woman in Timnah caught my eye. I want to marry her. Get her for me."* — ***Judges 14:1-2 (NLT)***

Most of us have been where Samson was. We're out and about, minding our own business, when *bam*! Out of nowhere, we see someone who catches our eye.

I still remember the day when a group of my high school friends and I went shopping at the mall and, as we were walking by one of the stores, I heard one my friends say, "Dude! She's hot!" Naturally, at that age, I turned to look and said, "Where? Who?" In other words, he had my interest piqued. Without hesitation, he said, "That one—the mannequin in the American Eagle window." I looked at my friend and said, "You need a girlfriend!"

For Samson, we can start to see it happening already. He didn't know anything about this lady, but he was so driven by lust that he declared, "I want to marry her. Get her for me." His emotions were affecting his ability to reason.

Now read what happened next:

> *As Samson and his parents were going down to Timnah, a young lion suddenly attacked Samson near the vineyards of Timnah. At that moment the Spirit of the LORD came powerfully upon him, and he ripped the lion's jaws apart with his bare hands. —* ***Judges 14:5-6 (NLT)***

At first glance, this is awesome! Samson was attacked by a lion, but because God had blessed him with unique strength, he literally ripped the lion's jaw apart with his hands. They didn't show that in *The Lion King*!

However, what looked like a blessing from God ended up being an issue for Samson. The wedding was all set up, so Samson traveled back to Timnah, the town where his fiancée lived.

> *Later, when he returned to Timnah for the wedding, he turned off the path to look at the carcass of the lion. And he found that a swarm of bees had made some honey in the carcass. He scooped some of the honey into his hands and ate it along the way. —* ***Judges 14:8-9 (NLT)***

Unfortunately, in scooping up the honey, Samson violated the Nazarite vow against touching anything dead. One vow broken, two to go.

> *As his father was making final arrangements for the marriage, Samson threw a party at Timnah, as was the custom for elite young men. —* ***Judges 14:10 (NLT)***

About to get married, Samson threw a party—but not just any party. The original word used here in Hebrew meant that he threw a feast, or a party for drinking. Essentially, Samson hosted a kegger for himself as a bachelor party. In doing so, he broke the Nazarite vow not to drink wine. Two vows down, one to go.

What happened next was a chain reaction of events, with one thing leading to another. Samson was marrying a lady from a different town, where the wedding was taking place. Since he didn't have any friends in the area, his soon-to-be wife's family hooked him up with thirty guys to hang out. According to his nature as a tough guy, he made a bet with these other men by making them solve a hard riddle. The guys couldn't solve it and got mad, so they made Samson's fiancée give them the answer. They won the bet with Samson–but then entered the emotion we all know best as anger.

> *...Samson was furious about what had happened, and he went back home to live with his father and mother. So his wife was given in marriage to the man who had been Samson's best man at the wedding.* —***Judges 14:19-20 (NLT)***

Emotions used selfishly cost us something. In this instance, anger cost Samson his desired bride. But I've also seen jealousy cause people to lose their friendships. I've seen fear hold people back from their dreams. I've seen disgust and judgment of others keep people out of the church. It's never pretty, and it almost always costs us something, even if we don't see what. Later in Samson's life, anger literally caused him to lose his hair and eyes, which broke his last vow.

If you took an honest evaluation of your life right now, would you say that your emotions are costing you something? The greatest news, however, is that God is a God of restoration.

Restoration

I'll admit that I go through stretches of time when I binge on house restoration shows, my favorite being HGTV's *Fixer Upper* with Chip and Joanna Gaines. I enjoy touring houses in general, but there's something awe-inspiring about watching a place that looks like it's meant for the garbage heap be brought back to purpose. It takes money and lots of hard work, but it's so worth it in the end.

The same is true of our lives. God is looking to restore everything that we've messed up. He wants to help broken relationships with a softening of hearts. With the right foods and exercise, He wants to heal our physical body that we've neglected. He searches for those who are spiritually dead to make them live again. He offers forgiveness of our sins to give us a new life through Jesus.

Maybe you're telling yourself: "Yeah but not me. That stuff happens to other people, but for me it's just too good to be true." Luckily for you, God specializes in too-good-to-be-true.

Control Your Emotions Before They Control You

My parents own two weeks of time-share for a condo in Florida, and that place became my main memory-maker for family vacations growing up. One experience specifically sticks out in my mind: It was spring break during my junior year of high school. We were on our way to the airport to return home to Indiana, and we were all hungry. We were standing in line at Burger King, and my brother, who was in college, was ordering just in front of me with his girlfriend.

As his girlfriend ordered Cini-Minis, the lady behind the counter let her know they were sold out, and my brother flipped out: "What do you mean there aren't any

Cini-Minis?!" I responded, "Dustin, they're Cini-Minis. Calm down, it'll be okay."

> *And "don't sin by letting anger control you."* — ***Ephesians 4:26 (NLT)***

I know I've seen sinful, controlling anger play out in my life, and I'm sure it's happened to you as well. But we can't afford to let our emotions control us. Instead, we need to develop a fruit of the Spirit known as self-control. Why? Because a life without self-control never lives up to its potential.

> *Better to be patient than powerful; better to have self-control than to conquer a city.* — ***Proverbs 16:32 (NLT)***

God has planned out an ideal life for you. No matter where you're at in your spiritual journey, God says you have great potential. In the words of Perry Noble, senior pastor of NewSpring Church in South Carolina, "You were created on purpose, for a purpose." But there's no way you'll live out your life to its fullest without the Holy Spirit developing self-control in you. The best-case scenario is for each one of us to learn to be led by God's Spirit and not by our emotions.

WORKBOOK

Chapter Three Questions

Question: What's an instance when you have let selfish emotion lead you to break a promise or to otherwise sin against God? What would have been a godly way to handle the situation?

Question: What is an instance when you have let anger control you? How should you have reacted differently?

Question: What is a first step you can take to lead a God-driven life instead of a selfish, emotion-driven life?

Action: Don't let fear, anger, or other selfish emotions control you. Instead, grow stronger emotionally by focusing on God's purpose and plans for your life.

This might take some work, but if you truly want to see your day's worth of emotions, try it: Use a notes app on your phone to note each time you experience a particular emotion, writing down which emotion it was. Do this for a couple of days and you might catch a specific emotion that is running your life. Then get control of it!

Chapter Three Notes

CHAPTER FOUR

Stronger Relationally

My mom has struggled with a lot of sicknesses over the years. As my dad says, "She got a lemon for a body." Late in 2014, she just couldn't kick this cold she had, and it continued to the point where she knew something else was wrong. After extensive tests, the doctors were able to diagnose her with C-Diff. Basically, our body has both good and bad bacteria inside it at all times, but her bad bacteria had overrun her good bacteria, which caused a serious strain on her health.

I vividly remember the phone call with her as I was driving down the road. I heard words that I never thought I'd ever hear come out of my mom's mouth: "I need you to donate some of your poop for me." Now, I tried my best not to wet my pants from laughter. After all, I'm sure this wasn't easy for her to say to me. I think my response was somewhere along the lines of, "Excuse me? Say again?" Of course, I followed this by asking,

"Why?" Because you don't just donate poop without asking why. At least I don't.

The doctors had a simplified answer for us: She needed an immediate family member who didn't live in her home to donate fecal matter so they could put it inside of her. My apologies if you're eating lunch right now. But it just so happened that I was entering one of my healthiest stages in my life, through eating right and exercise, so I became a prime candidate. The hope was that the good bacteria from my body would go into her body and kill off the excess bad bacteria.

A few days later, I traveled to a clinic across Indianapolis to get tested to see if I was a good fit to be a donor. I'm not the most patient person in the world at times, but lucky me, the computer system was down. After waiting for a lengthy amount of time and making a phone call to my mom to get her doctor to fax the order over, I finally got in.

They gave me a plastic pan to cover the opening in the toilet, two cups filled with chemicals, and a small plastic fork-looking utensil. I asked where the nearest restroom was, and they let me know that I couldn't do it there on the property. I couldn't believe it. You mean I have to leave and do this somewhere else? You had to be kidding me! Let's just say the Jack in the Box across the street got a visitor who didn't pay for food that afternoon.

But in the end, good news: I was a match. A week later, (even though I extremely dislike hospitals), I met my parents, donated my part, and then waited to see what would happen. A few days later, my mom was better.

This whole situation was by far one of the weirdest things I've ever experienced. Why go through it? Sure, one good reason is that I love my mom. But I also have this desire for the relationships in my life to grow stronger.

Broken relationships seem to be the new normal, and for some reason we are okay with that. Family members harbor bitterness for years because of harsh words spoken in the heat of the moment. Friends never speak to each other again because a rumor is assumed to be true. Co-workers don't want to be partnered together anymore due to a misunderstanding. A lack of trust exists between teens and their parents because too many promises have been broken over the years. And while I understand that these things happen, Scripture tells us there's a stronger way to do relationships.

Chapter 13 of Paul's first letter to the Corinthians has also been called "the love chapter" because it's so often used in weddings. And rightfully so, because it perfectly lays out how healthy relationships should function. These verses are loaded with relationship principles, but we'll focus on a few key examples.

Patience

Love is patient and kind. **—1 Corinthians 13:4 (NLT)**

Being four and five years old, my kids are terribly impatient. It pretty much comes with the territory. So I'm using it to my advantage and practicing my vocals. Currently, my singing ranks right up there with someone strangling a donkey, but fortunately my wife taught me a patience song that she learned from her mom growing up. Imagine this in a slow, deep monotone voice: "Have patience, have patience, don't be in such a hurry. When you're impatient, you'll only start to worry." So far, the kids still enjoy it and then forget what they wanted—so I sing it often.

It may not be pleasant when young kids are impatient, but it's downright sad when adults forget to be patient. I feel like saying this so many times: "An emergency in your life doesn't constitute one in mine." It's like some of us wake up and forget that everyone runs on their own schedule. Each person's job goes at its own pace. Each person's personality is different.

A crucial element of patience and other relationship principles is accepting the fact that life isn't all about you. Here's a healthy practice for us all: Once the patience song doesn't work any longer, if you find yourself starting to get frustrated, close your eyes and repeat this phrase until you're calm—"It's not about me."

Stopping the Drama

Love is not jealous or boastful or proud or rude. — **1 Corinthians 13:4-5 (NLT)**

One afternoon on Christmas break, a Delta airlines intern messed up their flight prices online. My wife and I happened to be two of many lucky recipients of dirt-cheap flight prices. How cheap? Try $75 round-trip tickets to Hawaii! To my surprise, more people seemed disappointed in the fact that we didn't help them get tickets, rather than being happy for our unexpected getaway.

When a spouse or friend gets something nice or has the opportunity to do something fun, there are two aspects to consider. First, don't be jealous. Our initial, selfish response is, "Why didn't that happen to me?" But rather we should be glad it happened to them—and we should voice our gladness to the other person! "That's so cool. I really hope you enjoy that." If you can't bring yourself to be positive about it, then jealousy is not only creeping in, but may also have set up camp already, and be causing constant issues.

The second aspect involves the "boastful or proud or rude" part of the verse. If you're the one who gets to do something nice or can afford to buy something new and impressive, don't rub it in. This includes excessive Facebook, Twitter, or Instagram posts of things you've bought, relationships you're in, or vacations you're on. There's nothing wrong with sharing things; the problem lies more in the way that you share. For instance, some people's entire online persona seems to center on flaunting a highlight reel of their life. Normal life can never live up to such a fantasy. If we catch ourselves putting on this kind of idealized display, we have to stop and ask what our purpose is. Is it to look better than others? Such an attitude is the mark of the boastful and rude mentality. Become more aware of your ulterior motives!

Flexibility

It does not demand its own way. — ***1 Corinthians 13:5 (NLT)***

Do you have that friend or family member who always has to have their way? Going out to eat, it's their choice or they complain. Going to a movie, they choose. It's honestly hard to make them happy, and it's not fun spending time with them. Now seriously consider: What if that's you?

It never ceases to amaze me that each year when it comes to Thanksgiving or Christmas gatherings, there are always one or two parties that want to serve a meal at three or four o' clock in the afternoon. For the sake of all the people who think like me—come on, man! That's just not normal. While it's not her fault at all, my wife always ends up with an earful from me. And it can be even more difficult to manage that when you have little kids involved. I remember feeding them fast food one year, shortly before arriving at the party.

Paul says there's a better way to live: Suck it up! It's time to stop being so difficult with each other. Yes, your way will almost always seem better than someone else's way, because you don't think like they do. But you don't always have to impose your way on others. Flexibility goes a long way in relationships. It shows that you care enough to give up what you want in order to join in with others.

Forgiveness

It is not irritable, and it keeps no record of being wronged. **— 1 Corinthians 13:5 (NLT)**

Keeping no record of wrongs—that's a steep hill for anybody to climb. But every hill climbed comes with its rewards. If we're honest, we read that and think, "What if I keep it to a short list of wrongs? If we forgive everything, isn't that just letting them off the hook?" I have heard it said that forgiveness is like setting a prisoner free, only to realize the prisoner was me. Forgiveness isn't about letting someone off the hook; unforgiveness, however, is a burden and stress that takes a toll on your life.

The children's minister and I were at lunch to talk shop about ministry and life in general. I was about to take my first bite when he threw out: "So, I need to apologize for getting on you the other day." I had no clue what he was talking about. "Let's just act like nothing ever happened," I suggested. I reminded him that if it was something that had bothered me, I would've said something.

I truly believe that a life of being completely honest with people and forgiving quickly is freeing. I don't have to remember whom I'm still mad at. I don't have to think about whom to get revenge on or whom to avoid when out in public. Offering lots of forgiveness and grace to others not only frees them, but also allows us to have a peaceful spirit.

Always Assuming the Best

> *Love never gives up, never loses faith, is always hopeful, and endures through every circumstance.* — ***1 Corinthians 13:7 (NLT)***

Relationships have this unique, unspoken dynamic: when we form relationships with other people, we have expectations even if we don't say them out loud. Call it unfair; it's simply what happens. But it's not like we can just whip out an expectations card every time we meet someone new. If we could, it might read: "If you're willing to be loyal, happy, encouraging, get me a birthday and Christmas present, give me good advice, and never talk about me behind me back, then sign here and we can be friends."

Now, of course we don't do this. People would think we belonged in the nuthouse. But that doesn't mean we don't expect those things. We expect our parents to love us no matter what. We expect our friends to never say anything that might hurt us.

But there's a gap between our expectations and real life, because people aren't perfect. Some closely related keywords run consistently through 1 Corinthians 13: "never," "always," and "every." If you notice, we use those same keywords in our expectations of others, but only in an unrealistic manner. Paul used them in a way that meets the reality of the broken world we live in. People make mistakes. They hurt us. We have to decide what we're going to put in the gap between our expectations of other people and real life—and love says we should always, *always* assume the best.

Assuming the best of others, no matter what, is an abstract concept. What does it look like? It looks like a family member who needs your help again, despite multiple trips to rehab. Or a friend who needs a favor after burning you on the last one. Maybe you hear a story that paints someone you know in a negative light. In all of these situations, you should assume the best of them. Andy Stanley stated it like this: "Love gives other people the most generous explanation possible."[5]

I firmly believe that partnering with parents as I minister to students paints the best-case scenario for each teen I work with. As you can imagine, over the years this has worked wonders in some situations, but has crashed and burned in others. One parent and I lost trust with each other through a couple of tough situations. We both eventually began to assume the worst of each other. On my end, I ignored phone calls. I tensed up when emails appeared in my inbox with the other person's name as the sender. My demeanor changed from genuine to fake while they were present in the youth building.

Looking back on this now, I'm obviously disappointed in myself. I'm sure I was wrong in some things, but even if I wasn't, by not reconciling this relationship I damaged all ministering opportunities for that family and that student. Assuming the worst led to a downfall that didn't have to happen.

What happens when we begin to assume the worst? You begin to assume your favorite team will always perform terribly. Or more significantly, you assume your thirty-year-old is never going to get their life on track, let alone move out of your house. When we assume the worst, life gets even messier. Many of us think that assuming the worst somehow protects ourselves from being hurt. We tell ourselves, "Well, I don't want to paint them into a picture that they can't live up to. And just in case the worst does happen, it won't seem so bad."

But the catch to assuming the worst is that you get results opposite to what Paul mentions in 1 Corinthians 13:7. You give up without a fight, you lose faith easily, hope fades, and you stop enduring hard times well. Paul reassures us that love is a better way to grow stronger relationships.

WORKBOOK

Chapter Four Questions

Question: What are the most important relationships in your life? What is the most you've sacrificed for these relationships?

____

____

____

____

____

____

____

____

____

____

____

____

Question: How specifically can you grow stronger in patience and flexibility?

____

____

____

____

____

____

____

____

____

____

____

____

Question: Whom do you need to grow stronger in forgiving? Whom do you struggle to assume the best of? And how specifically can you grow stronger in this respect?

____

____

____

____

____

____

____

____

____

____

____

____

Action: Grow stronger in your relationships by learning to demonstrate patience, avoid drama, be flexible, forgive others, and assume the best of other people.

Chapter Four Notes

CHAPTER FIVE

Stronger Mentally

Before finding those mistakenly cheap tickets, I never thought I'd get the chance to go to Hawaii. It was definitely on the bucket list, but I considered it one of the less-likely-to-happen items. The scenery was beautiful as expected, so my wife and I posted lots of pictures to Facebook.

But what you don't see in any of the pics is the absolute chaos that it took to get us there. We were on four different flights and missed several others that we were supposed to be on. We were awake for over twenty-four hours, which is hard while you do nothing but sit still in a seat. Then we arrived with no luggage to be found!

It all started in the Indianapolis airport. Our flight kept getting delayed there, which led to a domino effect. We landed in Minnesota only to realize that our other flight was already boarding, if not already gone, and my wife Angela was freaking out. I tried to hug her and tell her, "It's cool. Everything's okay." She responded with something to the effect of, "Get off!" She had that look in her eye, so I let go.

A few days later, I figured out why I had been so calm while the situation was driving her nuts: for Angela, getting to Hawaii would mean she was on vacation. In my mind, I was already on vacation.

Changing How You Think Changes How You Live

> *The church...became stronger as the believers lived in the fear of the Lord.* — **Acts 9:31 (NLT)**

The church—meaning every believer collectively, since the church isn't merely a building—grew stronger because they feared and loved Jesus. One area in which the church has played hands-off for too long has been mental health. Of course God wants to grow us to be stronger mentally, because many times the battle is won or lost in the mind.

> *Don't copy the behavior and customs of this world, but let God transform you into a new person by changing the way you think.* — **Romans 12:2 (NLT)**

So answer this question for me: How is God going to transform you into a new person? By changing the way you think. Changing how you think will change your behavior over time. It will grow you stronger mentally.

Let's say you hate Spam. I haven't eaten any in years, but my mom used to make some great fried Spam sandwiches. Even if you love Spam, pretend for a moment that you hate it, or replace it with a food that makes you want to gag.

So let's say you think Spam tastes horrible and has no nutritional value. The key word is "think." But if I could get you to think that you'd become rich, better-looking, and more likable if you ate Spam, I could get all of you to eat it! Every store within a mile of you would be sold out of Spam in a day.

In other words, if I change what you think about Spam, then your behavior toward Spam changes. What you think directly affects your life. What you think about over time takes over your life, either for good or for bad.

How do we win the battle for our minds? There are four ways in which we can make large strides toward victory.

1) Let God's Word change your thinking.

The first few times God put this book in my heart, I had all kinds of thoughts, very few of which were positive. "Jai, you had to be retaught basic writing skills in college because you were so bad at it in high school. What adult wants to read a book written by a youth pastor? And you're a young father—where will you find the time?" But then I remembered what Paul wrote:

> *For we are God's masterpiece. He has created us anew in Christ Jesus, so we can do the good things he planned for us long ago. —* ***Ephesians 2:10 (NLT)***

Day after day, I had to allow God's truth to replace my negative thoughts to get myself to where I mentally needed to be to accomplish writing my first book.

Ask yourself this question: "What have I not been able to do because of my thought life?" Now it's time to let God's truth replace the thoughts that are holding you back. The enemy loves our negative thought life and desires to keep us as slaves to our fallen minds.

King David knew the battle for the mind all too well. Being king, he had the world at his fingertips. While he witnessed great victories for God's Kingdom, his inner life was a struggle because of the plague that sin had produced in his life. His words in Psalm 119, however, reveal that he knew what he needed to defeat the ugliness in his heart and in his mind:

> *I have hidden your word in my heart, that I might not sin against you. —* ***Psalm 119:11 (NLT)***

David wanted to mentally know God's Word, but he didn't want to stop there, because information without application is useless. He wanted to more intimately know the Scriptures and to let them flow from his mind down to his heart. When this happens for us, it will change our behaviors and actions.

2) Don't believe everything that others think about you.

In the book of Jeremiah, we find a contrast between two different types of people: those who place their trust in other people, and those who place their trust in God.

> *This is what the LORD says: "Cursed are those who put their trust in mere humans, who rely on human strength and turn their hearts away from the LORD. They are like stunted shrubs in the desert, with no hope for the future."* —***Jeremiah 17:5-6 (NLT)***

People who trust in other humans and in human strength tend to believe what others say about them. Many have fallen victim to other people's thoughts about them, letting those thoughts and words become their identity. Maybe you've even dug yourself into what is called the performance trap. You keep trying to please others, thinking that you can earn their acceptance, only to be let down when it doesn't happen.

But God says we are cursed when we trust only in what others think of us. It will leave you dry and withered, with no hope for the future. Why? Because human thinking is flawed. We know finite information. We see life from a small perspective. God, however, created you on purpose, for a purpose, and wants the best for you. This is where the second type of person comes in—the person who fully embraces what God says about them:

> *But blessed are those who trust in the LORD and have made the LORD their hope and confidence. They are like trees planted along a riverbank, with roots that reach deep into the water. Such trees are not bothered by the heat or worried by long months of drought. Their leaves stay green, and they never stop producing fruit.* —***Jeremiah 17:7-8 (NLT)***

3) Don't believe everything that you think.

> *The heart is deceitful above all things and beyond cure. Who can understand it? "I the LORD search the heart and examine the mind..."* —***Jeremiah 17:9-10 (NIV)***

I'm not sure if I could even begin to count the thoughts that I've been wrong about in my life. I thought I could eat one doughnut for breakfast this morning. I was wrong. I thought I could make a horse run by whipping it with a stick—and I lost my four front teeth.

Each one of us has this broken, sinful nature that, if we feed more often than we feed our Spirit, would breed more deceit in our thoughts. We begin to think such thoughts as "I deserve this. I won't get caught. It's not that bad. I suppose it's okay to try anything once. Did God really mean 'Don't do that'?"

You wouldn't be reading this book right now if I believed everything I've ever thought. At one point in high school I thought about taking my own life because I wasn't sure if there was anything to live for. So don't believe everything you think, because your thought life might just kill you. Fill your mind with God's truth to fight off your own negative thoughts.

4) Guard your mind against garbage.

> *A wise person is hungry for knowledge, while the fool feeds on trash.* — ***Proverbs 15:14 (NLT)***

I know some of you have experienced the Netflix binge: choosing a show with several seasons available for streaming and then not venturing far from the television, other than for a quick bathroom break or to restock on snacks, as episode after episode plays. Before Netflix, the best way to do this was to get a couple of seasons on DVD or VHS. My personal poison was HBO's *The Sopranos*—God forgive me. In all honesty, after bingeing on several episodes, this show affected my thought life, changed the way I talked, and at times cultivated a deeply self-absorbed aspect in my life. Why? Because that's what I was feeding my mind: One swear word at a time, one "whack job" (the Mafia term for offing someone) at a time. It slowly corroded my thought life and changed my behavior until I realized it had to go.

Now it's gut-check time. Stop for a minute and ask yourself, "Am I hungry for knowledge like a wise person, or am I a fool who feeds on trash?"

The good news is that all of us at some point in our lives have fed on mental trash. We've all sinned against God—but you can find restoration. Scripture says that the penalty for sin is death, yet God sent Jesus to live a perfect, sinless life and to die in our place. He paid your penalty so that you'd be forgiven.

Once you understand that, you decide to follow Him because of what He's done for you. You get baptized and He equips you with the Holy Spirit to help you grow stronger spiritually until the day you die and go to be with Him in heaven. And until then, you can live a stronger life now. We should all come to want what King David desired when he sang this Psalm:

> *I will be careful to live a blameless life—when will you come to help me? I will lead a life of integrity in my own home. I will refuse to look at anything vile and vulgar.* — ***Psalm 101:2-3 (NLT)***

David desired to grow stronger mentally because it would honor God. He refused to let the filth of this world corrupt his mind or, ultimately, his heart. And he knew he could only do this with God's help, so he asked God, "Will You come help me?"

What he said next, however, was even more profound: "God, if You do Your part, I'll do my part." Since starting to work in the church, I can't tell you how many people I've seen resort to directly blaming God when things go sideways in their life. They refuse to take ownership of their own actions. David was wise enough to realize that God would do His part, but that it was up to him to control the junk coming into his life. And the same goes for us.

To allow God to develop you to be stronger mentally, what's one piece of mental trash you would be willing to remove from your life, starting now? Here's what I want you to do: grab a sticky note and a pen, then write down the piece of mental garbage that you don't want in your life anymore. And I want you to get specific. Maybe don't write down "TV" in general, but write down a specific show that you like, yet deep down know isn't good for you to mentally grow stronger. Or maybe don't write down "Internet," but rather the specific website that's harming your thoughts, or that band that warps your mind. Place that sticky note near the area where you need it the most for one week and then throw it in the trash. Take a second sticky note and write, "Romans 12:2—renew my mind."

The healthiest way to take this one step further is to add accountability. Find a trusted friend or a small group to share your efforts with and give them freedom to ask you the hard questions. Hard questions and honesty are the only way accountability works.

The Mighty Tree

I love big trees. They bring me a strange sense of peace. Around Thanksgiving time in our house, the battle starts between my wife and me over what kind of Christmas tree we are putting up. She wants a formal tree with white lights, fancy bulbs, and ribbons. I want multicolored lights with random ornaments from our childhood, including whatever our kids make at preschool. Angela has been gracious enough to let me win this battle every other year, for eleven years of marriage now.

Next year, however, that's going to change. After last Christmas, I bought a second tree for the kids and me. The variety of Christmas trees was quite overwhelming, from small to tall and thin and full. But I wanted something impressive—a symbol of strength. The year 2016 will be the year of the seven-foot-tall orange Christmas tree!

Please hear my heart on this, because it may come off as sounding conceited: I get one chance at this thing we call life. One! And I plan on resembling the mighty tree planted by the riverbank, soaking up all of the nutrients that God has to offer. I plan on producing fruit with my life. Give me a choice between the dried-up shrub and a big, strong tree and I'm choosing the big, strong tree every time. And I believe you should, too.

Choosing faith in God doesn't mean playing the weakling role; it's actually a faith that involves great strength and mental discipline. And God wants that for you. He created you for it. So stop living by what others think of you and take the best that God has to offer.

WORKBOOK

Chapter Five Questions

Question: How does God's Word affect the way you think? How can you grow stronger and more confident in your identity in Jesus?

____

____

____

____

____

____

____

____

____

____

____

____

Question: How do you let the thoughts of others affect you? Do you have these thoughts yourself?

Question: What mental trash do you need to remove from your life, and how can you get rid of it?

Action: Becoming stronger mentally requires letting God's Word change the way you think. Don't believe everything others think about you or everything you think about yourself. Instead, remove the mental trash from your thinking and find other people to hold you accountable.

Chapter Five Notes

CHAPTER SIX

Stronger Financially

We all experience major life-changing events. One of mine came somewhere around eighth or ninth grade when my family went on a mission trip with our church to Mexico. It was life-changing for me for several reasons, but I distinctly remember one van ride we took.

I sat looking out the window at a very unfamiliar scene—hardly any grass or trees, or anything green for that matter, which was strange for a kid growing up in Indiana. Then, as we went around the corner, I couldn't believe my eyes: It was a cardboard box village. I'm not joking. One cardboard box stood alongside another and yet another, and it seemed to stretch on forever.

I vividly remember the thoughts going through my mind: "I can't believe people live like this. These people have nothing." Seeing that kind of poverty firsthand changed the way I see life still to this day.

If we profess that Jesus is our Savior and we follow Him, then He wants to stretch us, challenge us, and grow us to be stronger in the different areas of our life—one of which is our finances.

Believers in Jesus too often doubt that God truly cares about finances. After all, money seems so "unspiritual"! Some people are especially cynical about pastors who preach about being strong financially; they assume the ulterior motive is to encourage bigger tithes and offerings to the church. But here's the truth: At the end of the day, God doesn't need your money to grow His Kingdom. Moreover, even if you think you're poor, it's crucial that you see the difference between the way the world views money and the way God sees money.

The world's way is to make every dollar that we can—to get a better college degree, work harder, and do everything possible to get more money. Why? So we can have nice things, of course! Or so we can impress people with our bigger house, more expensive car, or bigger savings account. Some of us pursue wealth because it gives us an adrenaline rush that we need again and again. In such ways, many people think money will make us happy. But I'm proposing to you that there is a better approach to your financial life.

Realize How Rich You Are

How much money would you need to consider yourself rich? Some people define being rich as having enough money to live a life of leisure;[6] for others, "rich" just defines anyone who has more money than they do.[7] But honestly, most of us aren't starving and don't have to think about where our next meal is coming from. We know a bed is waiting for us at home tonight. We have people who care about us and help us through life. The first step in becoming stronger financially is deciding in your head and in your heart to believe that you are already rich in many ways.

I love how King Solomon defines being rich in the book of Proverbs:

> *The blessing of the* LORD *makes a person rich...* — **Proverbs 10:22 (NLT)**

One of the richest guys to ever live said that money doesn't make you rich! Rather, God's blessing is the deciding factor, and God blesses each of us with more things than we can count.

The second part of the verse can seem confusing at first glance:

> *...and he adds no sorrow with it.* — **Proverbs 10:22 (NLT)**

Here Solomon is indirectly pointing out that financial wealth comes with the burden of management. The more money you have, the more God will hold you accountable for how you help manage the resources of the world. But with the blessings God gives us, there's no burden or "sorrow" attached. He offers us straight-up joy!

Hold On Loosely

During my senior year of high school, my family and I went to Miami, Florida, on vacation over spring break. But as we were standing in the Indianapolis airport, gathered like cattle around the luggage terminal and waiting for our baggage, I remember an awkward feeling come over me. ’Round and ’round the conveyer belt went as I stood waiting for my bag—suitcase, suitcase, guitar case, underwear—wait, was that my underwear? And were those my shirt and my shoes? I started freaking out! My whole suitcase was unzipped and open for the world to see. And worst yet, my PlayStation 2 was gone.

But Scripture offers us this admonishment in such moments:

> *For everything comes from him and exists by his power and is intended for his glory.* — ***Romans 11:36 (NLT)***

The key word here is “everything.” What comes from God? Everything! We have to hold onto our things loosely. As Paul wrote, it’s all God’s anyway. No matter what we’re clinging to, it’s only temporary and it comes from God. This is true of money, material possessions, and even people. As much as I love my kids or my wife, ultimately they are God’s and I have to hold onto them loosely, knowing that God is the one in control.

Share Generously

One story that forever changed my thinking about money was about a minister from California named Francis Chan.[8] As a minister of a mega-church who also made money off of book sales, Francis owned a large house and lived the easy life, as he called it. However, one day he and his wife decided to sell their big house and move into a smaller one. Staff members and congregants from the church started giving them a hard time: "We can't believe you're doing this. Why are you selling such a nice home? Doesn't your family deserve it? Think about your kids. Don't they deserve it?"

Francis's response was, in effect, "We *are* thinking about our kids. We are trying to show them what true generosity is, and to do that we need to sell our big house and move into a smaller one. That way we have the extra income to help others who are in need."

Francis Chan's sacrifice is an excellent example of the voluntary, cheerful giving to which the Scriptures encourage us:

> *You must each decide in your heart how much to give. And don't give reluctantly or in response to pressure. For God loves a person who gives cheerfully. —* ***2 Corinthians 9:7 (NLT)***

It's only from God that we receive anything, but he blesses us with money and possessions so that we can bless others in turn—not to store up material things and enlarge our bank accounts.

God wants to use you and your money to make a difference in other people's lives. But according to this verse, He doesn't want to guilt anyone into it. He wants us to do it because our hearts are in the right place. He wants us to give back to Him and His children because of what He has done for us. Giving isn't a matter of wealth, it's a matter of willingness. Are you willing to use what you've got?

And it's not all about money, either. For example, I save almost every cardboard box I come across—not to be a hoarder, but because almost every few months, someone I know decides to move and could use the boxes. It's one small way I give.

Use Money Wisely

The wise man saves for the future, but the foolish man spends whatever he gets. — ***Proverbs 21:20 (TLB)***

There was a major difference between my brother and me in high school. I can remember my brother reading books about how to save your money and how to get rich. By contrast, during my first year working at a grocery store, I had nothing to save for, so my friends and I would go up to the mall and waste our money on clothes, CDs, and video games.

Are you a saver or a spender? Most of us can answer this question readily. If you're a spender, you enjoy buying things just because you can. Perhaps you spend on credit because you've already spent beyond what you can afford. A spender desires to keep up appearances. A spender can't distinguish between necessities and luxuries. Count how many times in a day you say to yourself: "I need ________" (fill in the blank).

King Solomon calls a spender foolish. Why? Most of us in the United States don't truly need the majority of the material things we have, or the forms of entertainment we enjoy, to survive life on this planet. However, a hard time might be around the corner for you or someone you know. Do you want to be in the position to help or not? Our spending or saving habits will tell the truth for us.

A saver says no to the impulse buy, knowing something more important may come up tomorrow. A saver pays for things in full, without credit. The concept taught by many different financial advisors is "suffer now to live better later." In the long run, savers are going to be able to help themselves and others.

What You Have Versus Who You Are

If I asked you to make a list of what you'd be willing to do for $1,000, I wonder how it would differ from the list of what you'd do for $10,000. Many of us would try to reason this out: "Well, maybe I'd shave my head for $10,000, but not for only $1,000."

We may start with seemingly harmless examples like head-shaving, but such thought processes can all too easily lead us into a dark place. Would you sell your kid's favorite possession if offered the right amount? Would you steal from someone you love for money?

Would you cheat on your spouse for a price? What if there were a seemingly urgent, rational reason for needing the money? Ultimately, it doesn't matter: If we can be bought, then money, or whatever our motivation is—not God—is our master.

The scary part is that the idea of money can begin to push our moral boundaries of what's right and wrong. We might not believe that right and wrong have actually changed, but we become more willing to justify our wrongdoing because we receive money as a reward. In this way, we let money and our desire for material stuff determine who we are, when the Creator of the universe had already told us who we are.

> *For you are all children of God through faith in Christ Jesus...There is no longer Jew or Gentile, slave or free, male and female. For you are all one in Christ Jesus. —* ***Galatians 3:26,28 (NLT)***

You are a child of God, and nothing else in this life should affect your core identity. Ladies, you're daughters of the King. Guys, you're sons of the King. Nothing else in this life is more important than that fact.

No Fear

Do you remember "No Fear" T-shirts? These were popular when I was in junior high. No Fear T-shirts sported manly, tough slogans. One in particular declared, "The man who dies with the most toys, still dies." Those

T-shirts summed up a realistic view of why chasing money and material things simply isn't worth the effort.

We all need to see the reality of this: When you die, all of the money, all of the toys, and everything you've worked so hard to buy become meaningless. At that moment, when we stand before God and give an account for our life on earth, God's not going to ask you how much money you made. Instead, He's going to ask, "Did you know My Son, Jesus?" Because God ultimately knows that He has bought you:

> *You are not your own; you were bought with a price.* — ***1 Corinthians 6:19-20 (NIV)***

At some point in our lives, every single one of us was separated from God. To be honest, we were enemies of God because of the sin in our life. Scripture says that the punishment for our sins is death. But God loved us so much, He paid the punishment for us. He paid the highest price—the death of His Son Jesus. My prayer is that our financial priorities would line up with God's. Why? Because God has called our lives and our finances to something greater than this world had to offer.

WORKBOOK

Chapter Six Questions

Question: In what ways are you rich? What are the greatest blessings God has placed in your life?

Question: What possessions or people do you need to hold onto more loosely?

Question: How can you adjust your finances to make sure your priorities align with God's?

Action: Learn to appreciate how rich you are and how richly God has blessed you. Remember that God is the source of wealth of all kinds and He blesses us so that we can bless others in turn. Be a saver and a wise spender so that you're in a position to give generously and cheerfully to others when needed. Align your financial priorities with God's. Above all, don't let what you have define who you are.

Chapter Six Notes

CHAPTER SEVEN

Strong Physically

Angela and I have been married for about eleven years now, and about eight years ago we decided that I should get life insurance. I found this downright depressing. Who wants to sit around and prepare for what would happen to their family when they die?

Now, in high school I used to play about three to four different sports a year. But then college happened. I didn't put on the freshman fifteen (or forty), but my lifestyle changed drastically: lots of sitting and studying, but not much physical activity. And my food habits didn't exactly adjust to match my new sedentary habits.

A lady came to my office at the church and took my blood, and about a month later we got the results. To my surprise, smoking would have been the only way my health could have been worse. It was an eye-opening day for me. It finally sank in that my life needed to change when it came to choices I was making that affected my health.

Our personal health is important to all of us. So why don't our choices reflect this importance? One of our main problems is that we struggle to see the long-term results of the small daily choices that we make in how we treat our bodies.

But does God really care about your body—or am I just trying to get you to eat healthy and exercise because I do? To answer this question, we should first revisit the focal Scripture for this book:

> *The church...became stronger as the believers lived in the fear of the Lord.* —***Acts 9:31 (NLT)***

So far, we've delved into the concept of growing stronger in the areas of our emotions, our relationships, our Bible study, and our finances. However, we can't overlook the most tangible type of change that needs to take place—growing stronger physically. The importance of physical strength, or health, is abundantly clear from the story of Daniel.

As recounted in the book of Daniel, King Nebuchadnezzar of Babylon brought his army to Jerusalem and conquered it. This happened because God's people were being rebellious and not listening to His Word. They had walked away from Him. They had ceased worshipping Him. They weren't following Him with their daily lives. Therefore, God allowed them to be overrun by Babylon. As a result, God's people, including Daniel and his friends, found themselves serving the king of Babylon.

> *But Daniel was determined not to defile himself by eating the food and wine given to them by the king. He asked the chief of staff for permission not to eat these unacceptable foods. —* ***Daniel 1:8 (NLT)***

From the scripture above, we can see that Daniel was being wise in two ways: First, he knew what God's best was for his health, and was willing to stick to it. Second, he asked for permission rather than making demands. He was smart enough to know he'd have better luck with respectful requests than with hateful debates. There's so much the church needs to learn from Daniel in these regards, but we often seem to lack the necessary patience and humility.

One Choice at a Time

Growing stronger is a slow, daily process in all areas of life, but even more so with our health. There is no quick fix, even though we so desperately want there to be. Take a pill, change nothing about your lifestyle, yet lose weight? Yeah, right. Get a gym membership or join a sports team and become an instant athlete? Not exactly.

Accordingly, Daniel knew that if he and his group of friends made the wrong health choices day after day, it would take a toll on their bodies.

I played football from fourth grade through my senior year of high school. One week during my sophomore year, though, I threw up every day of football practice. If this happens to you, it's not normal!

My coaches called me into their office that Thursday after practice was over. I vaguely remember the conversation starting like this, albeit maybe a bit less blunt: "We've got a game tomorrow night. What the heck is wrong with you, Haulk? Are going to ralph on the playing field?" They asked a bunch of questions to try to determine if anything had changed in my life. We figured out that I was eating two iced honey buns before practice and my body was rejecting them.

This was just one example of a truth we all need to realize—that our choices affect who we become. We therefore need to take ownership of our choices. If you find yourself fifteen years into your faith, yet don't know Scripture or don't have a daily relationship with God, then you can't really point your finger at the church and say, "The church failed me." Was it the local church that failed you, or did you fail to make reading God's Word on a daily basis a priority? Over the years, have you taken the time to engage in open, honest conversation with God?

It's the same with our health choices: Who we are is determined by the choices we make. Put constant junk in, don't exercise, don't get health check-ups, and how can we seriously expect any result other than sickness and the weakening of our body?

Now God had given the chief of staff both respect and affection for Daniel. But he responded, "I am afraid of my lord the king,

> *who has ordered that you eat this food and wine. If you become pale and thin compared to the other youths your age, I am afraid the king will have me beheaded."* — **Daniel 1:9-10 (NLT)**

So we've got two points of view at play here. On one hand, we have the king's chief of staff, who thought Daniel and his friends needed to eat the royal food and drink wine to be healthy. This opinion reflected a highly cultured view of food and health in the Babylonian court. On the other hand we have Daniel, who claimed that God had already provided him and his friends with knowledge of the food they needed to eat to be healthy.

Ultimately, this passage isn't only about food, but also about their physical bodies. What did the chief of staff say at the end of verse 10? Effectively, he objects: "I can't have a bunch of pale, skinny guys running around the palace! You and your friends are supposed to be able to do battle if the king so orders, and it'll be my head if you grow weak!"

Both Daniel and the chief of staff understood something important that we need to think about today: Your physical health affects all of the other areas of your life!

Your physical health affects your mental health and how effectively your brain functions. It affects your relational health and your emotional health. It can even affect your financial health. Our physical health affects all of the other areas of our lives, but it's an area that the church has overlooked for years. This neglect can't continue!

No Change Without Challenge

"Hanger"—that is, getting "hangry"—is when you're so hungry that you get angry. It's your body's way of telling you, "I need nutrients *now*."

The other day I was driving my family down the road and my wife Angela started to lose it with the kids. If you don't have kids, then trust me that two kids under the age of five, confined in a van, can become a hostile situation—sometimes including projectiles. When the adults start to lose their temper as well, things can get truly ugly—and fast. My reaction, partly a matter of self-defense, was to declare, "Wendy's it is. Momma needs some food, kids. Don't worry, everything will be okay."

See how your health can affect your relationships and your emotions? It also affects your finances, because you can become addicted to particular foods and habits. Daniel's discussion with King Nebuchadnezzar's chief of staff demonstrated a clear understanding of the importance of proper health and nutrition:

> *"Please test us for ten days on a diet of vegetables and water," Daniel said. "At the end of the ten days, see how we look compared to the other young men who are eating the king's food. Then make your decision in light of what you see." The attendant agreed to Daniel's suggestion and tested them for ten days.* — **Daniel 1:12-14(NLT)**

Daniel was thinking, "Okay, so you're worried about how my guys and I are going to look eating vegetables and drinking water while everyone else feasts on the royal meals? Well, let's do a little test and then we'll compare at the end." But take notice that he set a very specific number of days for this experiment. Why do you think he did that? Because he knew that specific tests and specific goals are the ones that actually make a difference. Thus, Daniel's challenge was very detailed and specific, and they would only stick to it if it showed results.

Always remember that information without application is worthless. Would you change your habits for ten days to see how God strengthens your physical health? Below are some examples of tests with which to challenge yourself:

Drink only water.

Replace your side item for every lunch and dinner with a vegetable (especially a green one).

Do some form of exercise for a minimum of forty-five minutes. (Do something fun if that helps!)

Cut out an addictive habit of your choice that's harming your health.

This is where the rubber meets the road; there's no change without challenge. If you don't like my challenges, then create your own and push yourself. Just remember to be specific, as in my suggested challenges above. For instance, losing ten pounds isn't specific, but cutting out everything that has processed sugar is. And just as with any other goal, monitor for results.

> *At the end of the ten days, Daniel and his three friends looked healthier and better nourished than the young men who had been eating the food assigned by the king. So after that, the attendant fed them only vegetables instead of the food and wine provided for the others. —* ***Daniel 1:15-16 (NLT)***

It worked! Not only did they look healthier, but they impressed the attendant enough that he had to admit it was better for them than the indulgent food from the king would have been. The attendant saw what Daniel already knew: There are consequences or rewards based on how you treat your body.

Cocaine in Church

Let's say I walked on stage at my church and said: "Here you go, guys—tonight we're all going to do cocaine and heroin together! Wooo!" What would happen? I'd lose my job and be fitted for an orange jumpsuit before tomorrow morning's news even came on! My ministry, and many things in my life as we know it, would be over.

By contrast, if I walked in and laid out several boxes of doughnuts, as I do from time to time, no one would blink an eye. Yet the brain's response to cocaine is almost identical to our brain's response to the sugar in the doughnut. It creates addiction, a deep desire for more, which is a major consequence from which many people suffer.

Yes, the short-term consequence or reward based on how you eat, drink, or exercise is of course going to be weight loss or weight gain. That's what most of us are worried about, but there's so much more to healthy living. More Americans die every day from obesity than from hunger! Obesity is the second leading cause of preventable deaths—*preventable* deaths, which means that obesity is under our control.

Managing Your Body

Managing things isn't new to us. We manage lots of things. I personally get annoyed at having to manage my vehicles, because I'm just not a big car guy. I never have been. But if I didn't go through the annoyance of changing the oil, then my family wouldn't be going anywhere.

One Sunday afternoon during youth group, my car got a flat tire. Luckily for me, my friend Shane patched the tire for me, but if I didn't take it to the shop the next day as he suggested, then I'd have a flat again in a few days. I may not like managing my vehicles, but I do it anyway. The same principle holds true for you and your body.

> *You say, "I am allowed to do anything"—but not everything is good for you. And even though "I am allowed to do anything," I must not become a slave to anything. You say, "Food was made for the stomach, and the stomach for food." (This is true, though someday God will do away with both of them.) But you can't say that our bodies were made for sexual immorality. They were*

> *made for the Lord, and the Lord cares about our bodies.* — **1 Corinthians 6:12-13 (NLT)**

This passage is focused on sex, but it shows how God cares about the way we treat our body. And you're the only one who can manage your body. The bottom line that Paul is getting at is that we weren't meant to be addicted to anything. And some of us are addicted to sugary drinks or other unhealthy food habits.

Ann Wigmore, a holistic health practitioner, wrote, "The food you eat can be either the safest and most powerful form of medicine or the slowest form of poison."[9] Managing your body may mean gaining knowledge from others on the right foods and exercises, but you're the one who chooses what goes in your mouth, and you must decide to get active. No one else can do those things for you.

No Limits

Food and living a healthy lifestyle have been a struggle for me since high school. Truthfully, my bad food habits go back to my childhood—but it was my own entire fault. My parents tried their best to get me to eat healthy things, but I preferred to sit at the table, not eating my vegetables, until they likely felt bad about making me sit there.

Ten years ago, after my first few years as a student pastor, I was fifty pounds heavier. I struggled to go up a flight of stairs without being winded. I was worthless after about 1:30 p.m. every day because my mind was foggy from the excessive fried food and soda at lunch. All I wanted was a nap because I felt so drained. And I thought that was normal for someone in his early to mid-twenties.

Today, I'm thirty-four years old. I have a wife and two five-year-olds. I exercise almost every day, even if it's just for thirty minutes. In the last year, I've eaten more fruits and vegetables than in my previous ten years combined. And as a result, my mind is so much more effective and I can readily accomplish things with my physical body that used to be a struggle. Overall, this is going to help me to be a more active husband and father, a minister with fewer limitations, and to live life without hesitation.

Here is my point, which is also the point Rick Warren makes in his book *The Daniel Plan*: Who you are becoming is more important than what you are doing now![10] I knew God was already using me to do some cool ministry things with children and teens—He was allowing me to do good. But He was also starting to show me that I have much more yet to do and I could either be limited because of my health or I could say, "No limitations, God. I've prepared myself. I'm doing my best to live a healthy lifestyle so that You can use me."

Your first challenge for your physical health is to choose one of the ten-day tests I listed earlier. But the next challenge addresses a particular obstacle that I've found when it comes to God and exercise: many people whom I talk to about these two areas of life (healthy food and exercise) mistakenly assume that they know what healthy food is and what exercise looks like.

So I want you to become a student of food and exercise. If you're a reader, pick up a copy of *The Daniel Plan*. New Year's resolutions are a flawed way of thinking. As if real transformation were a short-term project!

Decide today to grow stronger physically. Put together a plan to be healthy and then live the plan—meal after meal, workout after workout.

WORKBOOK

Chapter Seven Questions

Question: How has your physical health affected your emotions, relationships, mental health, and finances?

Question: In what ways do you need to change your eating and exercise habits?

Question: What ten-day challenge will you accept in order to grow stronger physically?

Action: Physical health and strength affect every other area of your life. Remember the story of Daniel and seek to honor God by growing stronger physically. Study good health practices, change your eating and exercise habits, and aim for lasting change over quick results. Grow stronger so you can serve God and others more effectively!

Chapter Seven Notes

CHAPTER EIGHT

Stronger Priorities

Picture yourself standing on an island. You're all by yourself and not happy with where you are. You can see, way off in the distance, the mainland where you really want to be—only you can't see how to get there. Apparently you missed the memo on where they built the bridge, because there's no bridge in sight.

This is often where we find ourselves when we're in need of change. We see where we are on the island, and we see the life we want (including needed changes) over on the mainland. Yet we're not sure how to attain that life, or else the thought of doing something about it is overwhelming. This state of uncertainty is so frustrating that it leaves many of us thinking that it's just easier to stay where we are and stick with what we've already got.

A better life isn't unattainable, but it only starts with being able to envision our new future on the mainland. If we can also make the specific changes needed to realize that vision, then we'll get there. Otherwise, we'll remain on the island.

For me, this is where grit kicks in. If I can see the mainland—if I can see what needs to change in order for me to experience a stronger, better life—I'm going to fight until I get there or until I get as close as I possibly can. Revisit chapter 1 of this book if you find yourself lacking in that kind of grit!

The only place grit alone falls short of the mainland is when there's no plan in place. What good does it do me if I see the mainland off in the distance and, because I'm full of grit, I simply jump off of my island and start swimming? I'll drown for sure. If I have a plan, swimming across might work, but I would be wise to build up my endurance first by swimming around my island every day instead of hastily diving into the open sea. Or maybe I need a boat to get across. With a plan, I'd look at all my options first. But if we fail to plan, we plan to fail.

Even from the beginning of creation, God had a plan. And both God and Jesus knew that plan. They knew mankind would walk away from them and down the messy, dark road of sin. They knew this would separate a holy, wholly good and triune God from His created and beloved people—leaving them on an island without help and without the ability to be in relationship with Him. Because God's goodness keeps Him separated from the evil of sin.

> *Taking the twelve disciples aside, Jesus said, "Listen, we're going up to Jerusalem, where all the predictions of the prophets concerning the Son of Man will come true. He will be handed over to the Romans, and he will be mocked, treated shamefully, and spit upon. They will flog him with a whip and kill him, but on the third day he will rise again."* — **Luke 18:31-33 (NLT)**

A plan should always start with the "why": "Why do I need to change this? What are my priorities in life that require this change in my life?" Jesus never strayed for a moment from His plan because He knew His priority—the salvation of all mankind—was so important.

What Is Your "Why"?

Before I became serious about getting healthy, my brain had already been processing what a healthy life looked like. I had made few small changes, but nothing consistent. Being healthy was more of a vague, abstract idea at the time. It felt good to think about.

Then the moment came. I was sitting on the beach in Florida. I was reading and relaxing with my wife while the kids were running around and playing in the sand with their grandparents. My thought process was this: "I know I should put the book down and get up to play with my kids, but I'm tired and on the downswing of a sugar crash from breakfast."

Finally, a light bulb went off: these two kids numbered second in my top three most important things in life: God, family, and growing the church. I had to do everything I could to help them not only now but ten years—and twenty years—from now. They became one of my major *whys* behind the changes that needed to take place in my life.

The "why" is what fuels our desire to make necessary changes. When we don't feel like getting out of bed in the morning, our "whys" make it happen. These motivators can also change as we go through different phases of life. So, for one season of life your spouse may be your why, but it can shift to your kids, your job, your health, a hobby, or a specific passion that God puts on your heart.

What is your "why"? What are your priorities? Is it your job? Is it your spouse or your kids? Is it being successful enough to provide your family the freedom to go camping or boating every weekend when the weather is nice enough?

If you look at your priorities and they don't create excitement inside of you, or maybe seem shallow or a bit selfish, it might be time for a gut check of what your life is really about.

Evaluate Yourself Honestly

> *At last he stood up again and returned to the disciples, only to find them asleep, exhausted from grief. "Why are you sleeping?" he asked them. "Get up and pray, so that you will not give in to temptation."* — ***Luke 22:45-46 (NLT)***

Jesus made an honest evaluation of the disciples and found them lacking. He personally had left them alone for only a few minutes and had simply asked them to pray so they would not give into temptation. I am sure He was a little frustrated—at least enough to repeat Himself.

We aren't privy to the Savior of the universe in the flesh so that He could evaluate your priorities face to face, but if you're a believer, He has given you His Spirit. It's up to you to listen to Him. Ask yourself these three questions:

Question #1: "What's missing?" Is there something in this area that is completely gone from your everyday life, such as reading Scripture daily, keeping a financial budget, or engaging in physical activity? We have to be honest enough with ourselves to realize that we've completely missed the boat in some areas.

Question #2: "What's broken and needs to be fixed?" Maybe you didn't miss the boat; it's just broken down and in need of repair. For instance, your emotions are there, but maybe they're on a rollercoaster or always in a funk. Or maybe you have connections with friends and family but those relationships seem to be strained most of the time. If you really want to know the truth for questions 1 and 2, ask the people closest to you to answer them for you.

Question #3: "What's my next step?" This is the action step that puts in place what's missing so you can repair what's broken. This question is likely going to take more work on your part to answer. You may need to search out and read a couple of books on the subject. You may have to invest in a class, mentor, or trainer in the given area. Next steps toward true change aren't always easy.

Daily Habits Prove Your True Priorities

At first, I wondered why the disciples fell short of Jesus's expectations. After all, they were only napping, yet it seemed as if He was disappointed in them. However, when you put together what Jesus was doing (praying) versus what the disciples were doing (sleeping), we see that their habits showed where their focus was.

> *He walked away, about a stone's throw, and knelt down and prayed, "Father, if you are willing, please take this cup of suffering away from me. Yet I want your will to be done, not mine." Then an angel from heaven appeared and strengthened him.* — ***Luke 22:41-43 (NLT)***

Time and time again, Jesus practiced daily habits that kept Him connected to the Father: He prayed. He read the Old Testament. Many times, He would practice these habits in the morning while it was still dark out to limit distractions. The timing allowed Him to stay focused on His priorities. A plan leads to new daily habits when implemented, and habits lead to life change. But what does developing the right habits look like?

If you're an impulse buyer and that has hurt you financially, develop the habit of making a list before you ever go into any store. And until your impulses are under control, never stray from the list. Stick to the list!

If you plan to get physically healthy, your daily eating and exercise habits need to line up with that plan. If the changes aren't daily, they won't become habits and they won't stick. For instance, I make sure that I daily consume both fruits and vegetables. I've scheduled my exercise times as if they are work meetings that I can't miss. They are habits in my life that show my priorities.

If your spiritual journey is struggling, I can all but guarantee you it's because of your daily habits. Challenge yourself to thirty days of starting your day off with twenty to thirty minutes of reading and studying a devotional and your Bible. The more something takes place on a daily basis in your life, the stronger you grow in it.

This concept seems simple enough—but if our day-to-day habits don't line up with our priorities, then we don't really believe in our priorities. If we did, our behavior would follow.

Keeping Distractions in Check

Over His time with the disciples, Jesus continually laid out what should be their priorities in life, and at times evaluated them, but they kept getting distracted.

> *When the other disciples saw what was about to happen, they exclaimed, "Lord, should we fight? We brought the swords!" And one of them struck at the high priest's slave, slashing off his*

> *right ear. But Jesus said, "No more of this." And he touched the man's ear and healed him.* — **Luke 22:49-51 (NLT)**

Unless you have Mafia connections, your friends might not be distracting you by looking to hack someone's ear off. Nonetheless, it's important for us to stop every now and then to reflect on what might be distracting us from the priorities we consider most important. It could be the cell phone or tablet constantly in your hand. It might be a friend or family member. Managing distractions doesn't always have to come down to cutting someone or something out of your life completely, but it requires you to identify potential distractions and put boundaries on them.

Both my family and my church staff, for example, have enjoyed the Chick-fil-A cell phone challenge.[11] Everyone who participates gets a free small ice cream if they go the whole meal without touching their cell phone. In such simple ways, you can begin putting boundaries on your distractions as well.

The Power of Positive Thinking

Shortly after Jesus was arrested, He went through trial after trial. The disciples were wrestling through what this meant for them because they believed Jesus was supposed to establish an earthly kingdom with them by His side. Therefore, they initially saw Jesus's final moments as the end of a movement—a failure.

> *By this time it was about noon, and darkness fell across the whole land until three o'clock. The light from the sun was gone. And suddenly, the curtain in the sanctuary of the Temple was torn down the middle. Then Jesus shouted, "Father, I entrust my spirit into your hands!" And with those words he breathed his last.* — ***Luke 23:44-46 (NLT)***

What the disciples saw as a failure was in fact Jesus's greatest success! But even for Jesus, it was a process getting there. He had to endure many dark moments of feeling overwhelmed, abandoned, and frustrated.

One of my most significant valleys was when I was let go from a church. The youth and children's ministry at that church was my first ministry, but both the church leadership and I realized that children's ministry wasn't my passion. As a result, I was encouraged to pursue only youth ministry—which I did, but not before enduring the challenge of being laid off for an extended period. During those fourteen months, I questioned my calling to ministry, God's purpose for my life, and my identity.

So many times, what we see as failure is simply God's way of growing us. It's a pruning process that's necessary for our next steps in our transformation, though it's during these moments that our thoughts become critical. We have to fight the urge to get overly carried away with our emotions, because in our emotions we make mistakes. Instead, we must stand on the truth that God works everything for the good—so long as we're living according to His purpose (Romans 8:28).

During this process, it's extremely important that we forgive ourselves for the valleys. God takes the time to point out our flaws, and we have to wrestle through it, but such trials serve a purpose. Paul states that they help us develop endurance, character, and hope (Romans 5:3-4). Just don't get stuck in them!

This is where positive thoughts come in. It can be extremely hard to pick ourselves up and get back to our plans for growing stronger, but doing so is what's best for our lives. Jesus didn't die on the cross for us to stay stuck where we are, but rather to build a bridge and help us run across to the mainland! He came to give each one of us hope and a better life—both now on earth and eternally in heaven.

Take Time Seriously

At a leadership conference on family, one statement in particular impacted me greatly: Andy Stanley said that "you take time more seriously when you visually see it pass you by." After I got home from the conference, I bought two large glass vases and several hundred marbles. Then I calculated how many weeks I had from that very day until the week my kids would graduate from high school. I put that many marbles in the first vase and left the second vase empty. Every Monday morning since, I've taken a marble from the full vase and transferred it to the other, representing one more week that has passed.

Some might find it depressing to visualize their kids' lives pass them by, but for me, it reminds me to stay focused on investing in my kids because time is short. And more importantly than leaving a material inheritance, I want to leave them with a legacy of faith to pass on to my grandkids. My bottom line in life has always been to leave this world a better place than I have found it.

> *Teach us to realize the brevity of life, so that we may grow in wisdom.* — ***Psalm 90:12 (NLT)***

Ultimately, each one of us must keep in mind that our days are numbered. This realization can seem morbid, but nothing will ever change the fact that one out of every one people dies. It's a fact.

Our goal isn't simply to grow stronger in the different areas of life for the sake of growing stronger, but rather to make the best use of the time we are given. It's a way of honoring God and thanking Him for the life He has given to us.

So dig deep and get gritty! Don't give up! You can grow stronger in any area of your life if you truly desire to change and are willing to apply your growing knowledge to develop the daily habits that support your priorities.

With this understanding in mind, determine to grow stronger, be stronger, and live stronger!

WORKBOOK

Chapter Eight Questions

Question: What are your "whys"? Describe a "why" moment you've had. List your motivating priorities in life. Are there any priorities you need to add or remove?

____

____

____

____

____

____

____

____

____

____

____

____

Question: Do an honest self-evaluation (you might need to use the Notes page in this workbook section for additional space). List out the different areas of strength that we've explored in previous chapters of this book: grit, spiritual, emotional, mental, relational, financial, and physical. Then, next to each area, write out the three questions and answer them: (1) What's missing? (2) What's broken and needs to be fixed? (3) What's next?

Question: What distractions from your priorities do you struggle with? How can you keep those distractions in bounds?

____

____

____

Action: Apply your grit to setting priorities and living them out through your daily habits in every area of life. Perform an honest evaluation of yourself in the areas this book has addressed. Develop daily habits that reflect your priorities—your "whys"—and will allow you to live them out more fully and effectively. Find ways to keep distractions within bounds. Remember to think positively, but avoid complacency. Instead, take time seriously, dig deeper, and live stronger!

Chapter Eight Notes

CONCLUSION

Stronger—Day by Day

Growing in your faith is a daily process, not a one-time project. To get better at anything, you must become stronger in it. This requires time, practice, discipline, and hard work. The same goes for Jesus followers. After we accept Christ, He gives us the Holy Spirit to help us grow stronger in all areas of life.

Many believers think that just showing up to church on a regular basis means we're growing in our faith. But there's a major difference between church attendance and spiritual transformation.

We have to be willing to work the day-to-day process of growth: in grit, spiritually through our study of Scripture, emotionally, relationally, mentally, financially, physically, and in the way we plan and prioritize. This effort isn't a matter of fighting for our salvation, which is given freely. Rather, it's a matter of growing into stronger, more effective Christians for God's Kingdom.

In order to accomplish all of this, we must grow in our knowledge of God's Word and let it sink into our hearts for our actions to follow.

REFERENCES

Notes

1. King, Martin Luther, Jr. *Goodreads*. http://www.goodreads.com/quotes/26963-if-you-can-t-fly-then-run-if-you-can-t-run.
2. Duckworth, Angela L. "The Key to Success? Grit." *TED*. TED Conferences. 2013. http://www.ted.com/talks/angela_lee_duckworth_the_key_to_success_grit.
3. Roosevelt, Eleanor. "Eleanor Roosevelt Quotes." *Goodreads*. Goodreads Inc. https://www.goodreads.com/author/quotes/44566.Eleanor_Roosevelt.
4. Covey, Stephen. *The 7 Habits of Highly Effective People*. Free Press, 1989.
5. Stanley, Andy. *The Grace of God*. Thomas Nelson, 2010.
6. Hargreaves, Steve. "How Rich Is Rich?" *CNNMoney*. 9 August 2010.

http://money.cnn.com/2010/08/09/news/economy/wealth/

7. Ingraham, Christopher. "Americans Define 'Rich' As Anyone Who Makes More Money Than They Do." *Washington Post*, 13 March 2015. https://www.washingtonpost.com/news/wonk/wp/2015/03/13/americans-define-rich-as-anyone-who-makes-more-money-than-they-do/
8. Chan, Francis. *Crazy Love: Overwhelmed by a Relentless God*. David C. Cook, 2008.
9. Wigmore, Ann. "Ann Wigmore Quotes." *Goodreads*. Goodreads Inc. http://www.goodreads.com/quotes/563016-the-food-you-eat-can-be-either-the-safest-and
10. Warren, Rick. *The Daniel Plan*. Zondervan, 2013.
11. Cook, Gina. "Chick-fil-A Challenges Customers to Put Down Phones During Dinner." *NBCWashington.com*. 3 March 2016. http://www.nbcwashington.com/news/local/Chick-fil-A-Chicken-Coop-Challenge-370858981.html.

About the Author

Jai Haulk has spent his life investing in others. He married a great woman of faith named Angela over eleven years ago. They spent years desiring kids to be a part of their lives. God answered through allowing them to adopt two rambunctious and adorable kids, Isaiah and Lucy. They currently live in Fortville, IN. Jai enjoys hobbies such as playing golf, a variety of forms of exercise, reading, and challenging his kids to a wrestling match or race.

Jai is a graduate of Lincoln Christian University in Lincoln, IL, where his heart and mind was shaped by many men and women of God. Since then, he's served in the local church in the role of Student Pastor. He's experienced ministry in churches ranging from 70 to 2,600 members.

This is Jai's first book. He prays that it changes many lives, but only if it's by pointing people to Jesus. He understands that not everyone will agree on the viewpoints within, but desires to love everyone regardless.

About Sermon to Book

SermonToBook.com began with a simple belief: that sermons should be touching lives, *not* collecting dust. That's why we turn sermons into high-quality books that are accessible to people all over the globe.

Turning your sermon series into a book exposes more people to God's Word, better equips you for counseling, accelerates future sermon prep, adds credibility to your ministry, and even helps make ends meet during tight times.

John 21:25 tells us that the world itself couldn't contain the books that would be written about the work of Jesus Christ. Our mission is to try anyway. Because, in Heaven, there will no longer be a need for sermons or books. Our time is now.

If God so leads you, we'd love to work with you on your sermon or sermon series.

Visit www.sermontobook.com to learn more.